Cornwall

Compiled by Sue Viccars

Dedication
For my Dad.

Acknowledgements
With grateful thanks to all those who
came and explored Cornwall with me,
and especially to Brenda for her
support, and to Jane for sharing the
'odd' bottle of wine. Thanks are also
due to the National Trust Regional
Office at Lanhydrock for so willingly
supplying information for the original
edition.

Text:	Sue Viccars
Photography:	Sue Viccars
Editorial:	Ark Creative (UK) Ltd
Design:	Ark Creative (UK) Ltd

ISBN: 978-1-85458-517-2

While every care has been taken to
ensure the accuracy of the route
directions, the publishers cannot
accept responsibility for errors or
omissions, or for changes in details
given. The countryside is not static:
hedges and fences can be removed,
field boundaries can alter, footpaths
can be rerouted and changes in
ownership can result in the closure or
diversion of some concessionary
paths. Also, paths that are easy and
pleasant for walking in fine conditions
may become slippery, muddy and
difficult in wet weather, while stepping
stones across rivers and streams may
become impassable.
If you find an inaccuracy in either the
text or maps, please write to Crimson
Publishing at the address below.

First published 2002
Reprinted 2006, 2008, 2010.

This edition first published in Great
Britain 2010 by Crimson Publishing, a
division of:
Crimson Business Ltd
Westminster House, Kew Road
Richmond, Surrey, TW9 2ND
www.totalwalking.co.uk

Printed in Singapore. 4/10

Front cover: Coverack
Previous page: Pendeen Lighthouse

Contents

Keymap 1

SCALE 1:454 545 or 1 INCH to about 7 MILES *1CM to 4.5KM*

0 2 4 6 8 10 12 14 16 18 20 KILOMETRES

0 2 4 6 8 10 12 MILES

KEYMAP HEIGHTS SHOWN IN METRES

Keymap 2

SCALE 1:454 545 or 1 INCH to about 7 MILES *1CM to 4.5KM*

KEYMAP HEIGHTS SHOWN IN METRES

At-a-glance

1

Launceston

2

St Ives

3

Lanhydrock and the River Fowey

4

St Catherine's Castle

• Castle	• Artists	• Lanhydrock House	• Daymark
• steam railway	• Tate St Ives	• spacious parkland	• sandy coves
• museum	• sandy beach	• beech woodland	• coast path
• historic town	• coast path	• riverside walk	• historic sea port

Walk Distance
2¼ miles (3.6km)
Time
1 hour
Refreshments
Wide range of pubs and cafés in Launceston

Walk Distance
2½ miles (4km)
Time
1¼ hours (plus 1 hour)
Refreshments
Pubs and cafés in St Ives; café and restaurant at the Tate St Ives

Walk Distance
3 miles (4.8km) with optional 2½ miles (4km)
Time
1 hour (+ 1 hour)
Refreshments
Restaurant at Lanhydrock (fee, NT members free)

Walk Distance
2½ miles (4km)
Time
1½ hours
Refreshments
Cream teas at Coombe Farm in season; wide range of pubs and cafés in Fowey

---

Field paths sometimes muddy; steep climb up St Thomas Hill; non-dog-friendly stiles

Path through Higher Burthallan very muddy in winter; dogs to be kept under control at all times

Woodland tracks and paths, generally in good condition; dogs to be kept under control at all times, and only allowed in the river at specified places

Some long ascents on coast path, several stiles (not all dog-friendly); track from car park to **Ⓐ** very muddy after wet weather; dogs on leads through farmland

---

Walk Completed [ ]

Walk Completed [ ]

Walk Completed [ ]

Walk Completed [ ]

Cotehele

Trelissick

Tintagel

St Agnes

• Cotehele House • old limekilns • towering viaduct • chapel	• Riverside walk • superb views • ferry • park and gardens	• Ancient castle • stunning views • coast path • old chapel	• Mining remains • stunning coast • sea views • St Agnes Beacon
Walk Distance 3½ miles (5.6km)	**Walk Distance** 3½ miles (5.6km)	**Walk Distance** 3 miles (4.8km)	**Walk Distance** 3½ miles (5.6km)
Time 1½ hours	**Time** 1½ hours	**Time** 1½ hours	**Time** 1½ hours
Refreshments NT restaurant at Cotehele, picnic area at Cotehele Quay; Tamar Inn in Calstock	**Refreshments** Café at Trelissick; Punchbowl & Ladle pub in Penelewey (north west of Trelissick)	**Refreshments** Castle Beach Café (open all year) at castle entrance; pubs and cafés in Tintagel	**Refreshments** None on route; picnic area near St Agnes Head; pubs and cafés in St Agnes
Fairly steep path descent through woods to Cotehele Quay; dogs are not allowed within Cotehele garden	Well-surfaced paths throughout; big steps up from King Harry Ferry; steep ascent from **D** to **E**; dogs to be kept on leads in park	Coast path rocky and undulating; steep descent to Tintagel Haven; field paths sometimes muddy; dogs on leads through farmland; non-dog-friendly stiles	Track from **F** to **G** muddy in winter; many paths crossing St Agnes Beacon; dogs to be kept under control at all times

p.34
p. 38
p. 42
p. 46

Walk Completed ☐

Walk Completed ☐

Walk Completed ☐

Walk Completed ☐

9	10	11	12

The Lizard to Church Cove	*Veryan and Portloe*	*Porthcurno and Treen*	*Geevor and Levant*
• South point • coast path • lifeboat station • ancient church	• Old fishing village • roundhouses • country lanes • coast path	• Cliff theatre • sandy beaches • stunning views • cliff castle	• Lighthouse • tin mining • beam engine • mining villages
Walk Distance 3½ miles (5.6km)	**Walk Distance** 3½ miles (5.6km)	**Walk Distance** 3½ miles (5.6km)	**Walk Distance** 4 miles (6.4km)
Time 1¾ hours	**Time** 1¾ hours	**Time** 1¾ hours	**Time** 1¾ hours
Refreshments Polpeor Café and Wave Crest Café at Lizard Point: cafés and pub in Lizard village	**Refreshments** New Inn and Ellerkey Coffee Shop, Veryan; Ship Inn, Lugger Hotel, Portloe	**Refreshments** Porthcurno Beach Café and pub at Porthcurno; café and Logan Rock pub in Treen	**Refreshments** Count House Café at Geevor
High and uneven steps down to and up from Housel Bay; *steep ascent inland* from Church Cove; dogs to be kept under control at all times	Field paths muddy in winter; dogs on leads through farmland; *steep climb* out of Portloe to Sunny Corner; coast path narrow and exposed round Jacka Point	Steep walk up lane to Minack; high uneven steps down towards beach; narrow and exposed path along Treen Cliff; dogs to be kept under control at all times	Undulating coast path from Pendeen lighthouse to Geevor, very muddy in places in winter; dogs to be kept under control at all times

p. 50	p. 54	p. 58	p. 62
Walk Completed	Walk Completed	Walk Completed	Walk Completed

13	14	15	16

Coverack	*St Anthony-in-Meneage*	*Mount Edgcumbe*	*Morwenstow*
• Old fishing village • raised beach • working quarry • delicious icecream	• Riverside path • sandy coves • coastal headland • beautiful church	• Plymouth Sound • zigzag path • gardens • Empacombe	• Hawker's Hut • church, vicarage • spectacular cliffs • rolling farmland
Walk Distance 5 miles (8km)	**Walk Distance** 5 miles (8km)	**Walk Distance** 5½ miles (8.8km)	**Walk Distance** 4½ miles (7.2km)
Time 3 hours	**Time** 2 hours	**Time** 2½ hours	**Time** 2½ hours
Refreshments Paris Hotel and Wave café in Coverack; Croust House restaurant at Roskilly's	**Refreshments** The New Inn and South Café, Manaccan; icecream shop at St Anthony-in-Meneage	**Refreshments** Edgcumbe Inn at Cremyll, Orangery Restaurant in Mount Edgcumbe Gardens	**Refreshments** The Bush Inn at Crosstown; Rectory Farm Tearooms at Morwenstow
Parts of coast path wet and boggy all year round; *demanding climb inland from* **C**; dogs to be kept under control at all times	Relatively easy coast path; some paths muddy after rain; dogs to be kept on leads through Bosahan estate and farmland	*Steep descent to Millbrook creek, sometimes slippery; part of coast path has steep ascent/ descent (steps);* dogs on leads in Country Park, and to be kept under control at all times	*Very steep ascents/descents on coast path and some exposed sections;* dogs to be kept on lead through farmland, and under control at all times
p.66	**p. 71**	**p. 75**	**p. 80**
Walk Completed ☐	Walk Completed ☐	Walk Completed ☐	Walk Completed ☐

17

Lamorna and Mousehole

18

St Anthony Head

19

Trevone and Stepper Point

20

Port Quin to Port Isaac

• Wonderful cove • nature reserve • fishing harbour • cliff terraces	• Tidal creek • sailing boats • wildflowers • lighthouse	• Tortured coastline • daymark • estuary views • great geology	• Rocky coves • rolling farmland • fishing village • coast path

Walk Distance
5 miles (8km)
Time
3 hours
Refreshments
Lamorna Wink pub and café, Lamorna Cove; pubs, cafés in Mousehole

Walk Distance
6½ miles (10.5km)
Time
3 hours
Refreshments
Royal Standard pub, Gerrans; Plume of Feathers pub, Portscatho

Walk Distance
6½ miles (10.5km)
Time
3 hours
Refreshments
Madrips beach café, Trevone beach; Well Parc pub, Trevone

Walk Distance
6½ miles (10.5km)
Time
3 hours
Refreshments
The Golden Lion pub, cafés and restaurants in Port Isaac

Scrambly coast path, with big rocks, steps and wet patches; *steep descent to/ascent from Mousehole on lane;* inland fields boggy in wet weather; keep dogs on leads

Some paths muddy after wet weather; some dog-friendly stiles on coast path, some not; dogs on leads through Place conservation area; *very steep climb from St Anthony lighthouse to* **E**

Take care on coast path Trevone to Stepper Point (unfenced and high cliffs); beware Round Hole at Trevone; dogs on leads; non-dog-friendly high Cornish stiles

Dogs to be kept on leads through farmland; *strenuous coast path, with steep ascents/descents and long flights of high steps; parts slippery after rain*

p. 84	p. 89	p. 94	p. 99

Walk Completed ✓

Walk Completed ☐

Walk Completed ☐

Walk Completed ☐

Introduction

For many, Cornwall is the ideal holiday destination. Characterful fishing villages; colourful local customs and folklore; wide sandy beaches and rugged cliffs; peaceful wooded estuaries and wild moorland; a place of family holidays, of sunshine, icecream and pasties. But just scratch beneath the surface and you will discover the real Cornwall, a land steeped in history and tradition with a remarkable industrial heritage.

Cornish choughs

The Cornish people have a fierce sense of independence born of a physical remoteness from London, the traditional seat of power; of a centuries-long history of oppression and hardship; and of a unique social heritage. There is a wealth of prehistoric evidence here, starting around 3000BC when Neolithic peoples constructed megalithic chambered tombs. Bronze Age peoples erected stone circles and standing stones on the bleak inland moors. The Iron Age produced compact villages, such as Chysauster, and the unusual 'fogous', granite-lined underground 'passages' unique to West Penwith and the Isles of Scilly, whose exact use is unresolved; and also fortified cliff castles perched high above the sea, such as that at Treryn Dinas.

The tradition of castle building continued in the Norman period, as evidenced by castles at Launceston and Lostwithiel (Restormel); in the 13th century major refortification was carried out at Tintagel, where – as legend has it – King Arthur was plucked from the sea as a baby. Henry VIII was responsible for the later splendid castles overlooking the wide river estuaries of the south coast, such as those at Pendennis (Falmouth) and St Mawes, part of his defence system in the face of possible invasion from France. The county also has her fair share of fine houses, many of which, with their gardens, are now open to the public – Lanhydrock, near Bodmin, is said to be one of the best examples of a late Victorian country house in Great Britain.

Life has always been hard here. Those involved in the traditional ways of earning a living – fishing, mining the natural resources of tin and copper, and small-scale farming – have had to adapt to shifting fortunes over the years. Despite occasional (and in one case, at South Crofty, on-going) attempts to revive it, the mining industry has now disappeared in the face of cheaper foreign imports. Cornwall is peppered with industrial memorabilia in the form of starkly beautiful engine houses, many of which have been restored. The demise of the fishing industry, only clinging on today in a few places such as Newlyn, has meant that those villages once reliant on fishing – such as Padstow, St Ives and Mousehole – have had to adapt too. Most now attract hundreds of holidaymakers, drawn by the narrow cobbled streets and picturesque settings – and, increasingly, the wealth of good restaurants, and of art and craft galleries. Cornwall has long been a mecca for artists, attracted by the rugged coastal scenery and superb qualities of light.

The county's equable maritime climate has strongly influenced another of Cornwall's great attractions: her gardens. Sub-tropical plants and flowers flourish in the sheltered valleys of the south coast, such as at Glendurgan, Cotehele and Trelissick; snowdrops and daffodils bloom earlier here than anywhere else on mainland Britain. And early this century the county hit the headlines thanks to the ambitious Eden Project, an inspirational development in a derelict china clay quarry near St Austell, where the visitor can wander through space-age biomes containing incredible plants gleaned from all over the world. So much more than a mere 'tourist attraction', this project attracts hundreds of thousands of visitors, many of whom have been encouraged to explore the area in more depth. Tourism now forms a vital part of Cornwall's economy, assisted by improved transport links with the rest of the country.

Playing 'Pooh Sticks' on the River Fowey at Lanhydrock

Walking in Cornwall

The majority of the walks in this book explore Cornwall's magnificent 500-mile coastline, and follow sections of the South West Coast Path National Trail. Readers should be aware that *the coast path is not a surfaced path and that sections may be rocky or muddy – and sometimes both!* An indication of the sort of terrain covered by the walk is given at the start of each route. Boots or strong footwear are recommended for every route, and *it is wise*

Lifeboat station, Kilcobben Cove

always to carry the relevant OS map (and know how to use it) and take waterproof clothing with you unless sunshine is guaranteed. Be aware too that great care should be taken if undertaking a cliff-top walk in windy or very wet conditions.

This book gives a taste of all Cornwall's attractions, both natural and man-made, through a wide range of walks to suit all ages and abilities, listed in order of increasing difficulty either in terms of ascent and descent, or terrain underfoot. There's a gentle stroll around historic and frequently bypassed Launceston, 'the gateway to Cornwall', with its impressive Norman castle and 14th-century church of St Mary Magdalene. Tackle a tough trek along cliffs of rare beauty and wild magnificence near Morwenstow, just inside the border with Devon – an area renowned not just for its natural power but for its history of smugglers and shipwrecks and the colourful Rev. Stephen Hawker, who resided over the parish in the 19th century. Explore picturesque St Ives, once reliant on pilchard fishing, then home to the 20th-century arts movement inspired by the likes of Ben Nicholson and Dame Barbara Hepworth, now setting for the Tate St Ives gallery that overlooks sandy Porthmeor beach in the centre of the town. You can wander along the wooded banks of the River Fal around the edge of the Trelissick estate, now in the hands of the National Trust, or glean a sense of Cornwall's working past on an exploration of the ruined mine workings on the coast at Geevor, which only finally closed in 1990.

There's no doubt about it: Cornwall is a beautiful, fascinating county, with superb natural scenery and a wonderful history, and has much to offer – and is best and most satisfactorily explored on foot!

This book includes a list of waypoints alongside the description of the walk, so that you can enjoy the full benefits of gps should you wish to.

For more information on using your gps, read the *Pathfinder® Guide GPS for Walkers*, by gps teacher and navigation trainer, Clive Thomas (ISBN 978-0-7117-4445-5).

For essential information on map reading and basic navigation, read the *Pathfinder® Guide Map Reading Skills* by outdoor writer, Terry Marsh (ISBN 978-0-7117-4978-8). Both titles are available in bookshops or can be ordered online at www.totalwalking.co.uk

Launceston

- Castle
- steam railway
- museum
- historic town

The historic town of Launceston, walled in the 12th century and 'the gateway to Cornwall', is full of surprises, and there's something of interest for everyone on this easy walk which leads from the heart of the old town to run through peaceful fields, with great views to the Norman castle above, and returns via the steam railway, museum and 16th-century church.

walk 1

View over the town from Launceston Castle

walk **1**

START Launceston

DISTANCE 2¼ miles (3.6km)

TIME 1 hour

PARKING Long or short stay car parks (fee-paying) on Race Hill

ROUTE FEATURES Field paths sometimes muddy; steep climb up St Thomas Hill; non-dog-friendly stiles

GPS WAYPOINTS

   SX 333 844
Ⓐ SX 333 842
Ⓑ SX 327 841
Ⓒ SX 327 849
Ⓓ SX 330 847

PUBLIC TRANSPORT Bus service from Barnstaple, Bude, Exeter, Liskeard, Okehampton, Plymouth, Tavistock

REFRESHMENTS Wide range of pubs and cafés in Launceston

PUBLIC TOILETS In the car park

PLAY AREA In Coronation Park; in Tredyan Road

ORDNANCE SURVEY MAPS Explorer 112 (Launceston & Holsworthy), Landranger 201 (Plymouth & Launceston)

Leave the car park and turn left up Race Hill. Take the first right (Bounsalls Lane), then immediately turn left up Windmill Lane (dead end). The lane ends at a turning area; walk ahead to enter Coronation Park Ⓐ, laid out as a pleasure gardens in 1895.

Turn left along the tarmac path and walk gently uphill, passing the railed-off Windmill reservoir, completed in 1895, on the left. Little is known about the windmill from which the reservoir takes its name. Leave the park between the children's play area and the

> **?** *There is a memorial to Leonard Macleod Hender in Coronation Park. How, when and where did he die?*

leisure centre, to meet the road opposite Launceston College, and follow the road right. Pass Windmill Hill on the right; cross over Dunheved Road (note the original Launceston College building on the left; the school was founded by Wesleyan methodists in 1873) and turn left. Follow the road right into Dunheved Fields, and the second right down Hendra Vale. When Western Road is reached, cross over with care and go down Carboth Lane to reach Chapel Ⓑ.

Cross the lane, and follow footpath signs over

a stile into a field. Turn left to cross another stile, then right. This is a lovely, gentle route along the bottom of the valley of Harpers Lake (stream) – a deer park in Norman times – with great views of

✻ The church of **St Mary Magdalene**, one of three in Launceston, is famed for its superbly carved exterior. The tower dates from 1380, and is the only feature remaining of the church built by Edward, the Black Prince. The present church was built by Henry Trecarrell in the early 16th century, to appease the souls of his ancestors when, tragically, he lost his family in 1511.

Launceston Castle opening up to the right. Cross another stile, then pass another to enter the final field, and through a five-bar gate onto a grassy track. Cross another stile, then head down the track and through a gate onto Wooda Lane, with allotments on the right, near the site of an old well – Maiden's Well.

Launceston Castle keep

Turn left; follow the lane until it meets Tredyan Road **C**; turn right to pass the children's playground on the right. Walk on to pass the steam railway on the left, a narrow-gauge line that runs along the Kensey valley as far as Newmills. Cross St Thomas Road (take care) and turn immediately right up steep St Thomas Hill. Cross Wooda Road at the top, and walk straight on up Tower Street; at the first bend to the left go straight ahead up wide railed steps to reach Castle Street **D**.

Turn right to pass the Lawrence House Museum (National Trust) on the right, a beautiful Georgian house dating from 1753 and built by Humphry Lawrence. The house was also the unofficial headquarters for French POWs during the Napoleonic wars, during which time

Launceston was a parole town. Reach the Eagle House Hotel on the right (with entrance to the castle ahead) and follow the road as it bears left. Keep ahead to find the Church of St Mary Magdalene on the left. Bear right down Church Street and into Southgate; one of the three entrance gates remaining from the time that Launceston was a walled town, Southgate was originally used as a prison. Walk up Race Hill; the car park is on the left. ■

The ruins of **Launceston Castle** rise proudly above the town, and date from soon after the Norman Conquest. Most of what can be seen today dates from the 13th century when the castle was remodelled under instruction of Richard, Earl of Cornwall. The castle (which has never seen active service – though it changed hands five times during the Civil War, without resistance) also marks the western end of the Two Castles Trail, a long-distance walking route linking the Norman castles at Launceston and at Okehampton over the border in Devon.

St Ives

- Artists
- Tate St Ives
- sandy beach
- coast path

walk 2

The popular seaside town of St Ives has drawn both artists and holidaymakers for many years, attracted by the fantastic quality of light, beautiful coastline and wonderful sandy beaches. You can experience a little of everything St Ives has to offer on this walk, which leads past the Tate St Ives gallery out to lovely Clodgy Point, and back to the bustling town via quiet tracks and lanes.

The Tate St Ives from Carrick Du

walk 2

START St Ives

DISTANCE 2½ miles (4km)

TIME 1¼ hours (plus 1 hour)

PARKING Barnoon upper car park (fee-paying), signposted for Tate St Ives and Porthmeor beach

ROUTE FEATURES Path through Higher Burthallan very muddy in winter; dogs to be kept under control at all times

GPS WAYPOINTS

- SW 516 407
- Ⓐ SW 515 408
- Ⓑ SW 507 412
- Ⓒ SW 504 411
- Ⓓ SW 503 408
- Ⓔ SW 510 405

PUBLIC TRANSPORT Tel. 01452 425543

REFRESHMENTS Wide range of pubs and cafés in St Ives; café and restaurant at the Tate St Ives

PUBLIC TOILETS Porthmeor beach

PLAY AREA None

ORDNANCE SURVEY MAPS Explorer 102 (Land's End), Landranger 203 (Land's End & Isles of Scilly)

Leave the car park by the locked public toilets and take the steps which lead steeply down to Beach Road, running along the back of Porthmeor beach. The Tate St Ives, built on the site of an old gasworks, can be found just to the right: this spectacular building, opened in June 1993, was designed and built by Eldred Evans and David Shalev. The gallery houses exhibitions of works produced by St Ives artists from the late 1880s to the present day.

One of the prime figures of the 'plein air' movement which drew artists to **St Ives** was Ben Nicholson (1894–1982), one of Britain's major abstract artists, who came here on holiday with fellow artist Christopher Wood (1901–30) in 1928. Nicholson moved here in 1939 with his wife, the sculptor Barbara Hepworth (1903–75). Over the next two decades they turned St Ives into one of the leading centres of British art.

Ⓐ Turn left; when the toilets are reached on the right, follow coast path signs along the tarmac walkway that runs below the road to pass Porthmeor Bowling Club, and on across a grassy area. Follow coast path signs to pass Carrick Du and a stone shelter; look back for fantastic views over The Island and across St Ives Bay to the lighthouse on Godrevy Island, eventually passing through a kissing-gate Ⓑ.

Glorious summer colour

Follow the cliff top path around the cliffs of Clodgy Point ('clodgy' means 'leper' in Cornish). Walk round the headland, and eventually up across Burthallan Cliff to rejoin the coast path and continue uphill, aiming for a footpath post (coast path signed right) **C**.

Leave the coast path and walk uphill. The narrow, grassy path soon bears right through bracken and gorse, and later between low walls, eventually to reach Higher Burthallan **D**.

Pass through a gate and onto a muddy track; look out for superb views over St Ives Bay to the left. The track becomes tarmac at Fairview Farmhouse; walk along the lane to pass the Garrack Hotel and meet the road **E**.

Turn left downhill, and follow the road towards the centre of St Ives. This picturesque old fishing town's original claim to fame was that it was Cornwall's most important pilchard-

> Nicholson and Wood 'discovered' local mariner and artist **Alfred Wallis** (1855–1942), who took up painting at the age of 70 to occupy him after his wife's death. His primitive paintings are some of the best-known from the St Ives School, yet this modest man never regarded himself as a 'proper artist'. His cottage can be found on the left of Back Road West, a little way past the Tate St Ives, towards The Island.

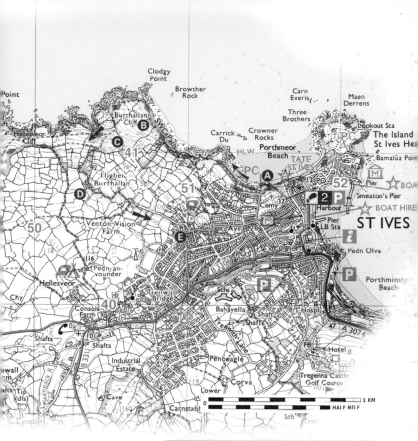

fishing port, until the
demise of the industry
in the early 20th
century. It is well worth

? *Across the road from the start of the tarmac walkway on point Ⓐ you pass an old well. To whom is it dedicated?*

exploring – down the long narrow lanes, courtyards and alleyways
between Porthmeor beach and the harbour – where (out of season) you
can get a real feeling of what life must have been like here in the 18th
and 19th centuries, before the holiday trade took over. Where the road
bends sharp right and downhill, cross over (with Barnoon cemetery on
the left) and go straight on to find the car park on the left. ■

Lanhydrock and the River Fowey

- Lanhydrock House
- spacious parkland
- beech woodland
- riverside walk

Imposing late 19th-century Lanhydrock House and its magnificent estate provide the focus for this walk, which runs along the lovely River Fowey, explores the estate's beechwoods and farmland, then reaches the house itself, set in sweeping parkland. An optional (yet easy) extension to the route leads to Restormel Castle, 13th-century symbol of Norman authority.

walk 3

Lanhydrock's impressive gatehouse

START Respryn Bridge

DISTANCE 3 miles (4.8km) with possible 2½ miles (4km) extension

TIME 1 hour (plus 1 hour)

PARKING National Trust car park at Respryn Bridge (locked sunset to sunrise, £2 honesty box), sign-posted from B3268 Bodmin (A38) – Lostwithiel

ROUTE FEATURES Woodland tracks and paths, generally in good condition; dogs to be kept under control at all times, and only allowed in the river at specified places

GPS WAYPOINTS

* SX 099 636
* Ⓐ SX 099 634
* Ⓑ SX 093 628
* Ⓒ SX 092 629
* Ⓓ SX 086 627
* Ⓔ SX 086 635

PUBLIC TRANSPORT Bus service from Bodmin (to Lanhydrock House)

REFRESHMENTS Restaurant at Lanhydrock (admission fee/NT members free); picnic benches along riverbank

PUBLIC TOILETS At Lanhydrock House (free); also at main car park (plus picnic area, plant sales) ½ mile back up lane from Respryn Bridge, then turn left

PLAY AREA None

ORDNANCE SURVEY MAPS Explorer 107 (St Austell & Liskeard), Landranger 200 (Newquay & Bodmin)

This walk can easily be done in either direction, but taking it clockwise means that you might arrive at Lanhydrock House in time for tea. Turn left just before the car park exit, then bear right up steps to the lane. Cross pretty five-arched Respryn Bridge, which dates from 1520.

> **Lanhydrock House** and gardens provide a fascinating insight into late Victorian wealthy country life. Now in the care of the National Trust, Lanhydrock is one of the most impressive 19th-century houses in England. Only the original 17th-century gatehouse and north wing survived a terrible fire in 1881, the remainder of the house being rebuilt at that time. The beautiful gardens were also laid out in Victorian times.

Over the bridge turn right to pass through a kissing-gate Ⓐ, and follow the River Fowey downstream. The river, which has its source near Brown

> *In what way did Spillers Foods help the Lanhydrock estate, and when? You will find the answer on a seat some-where along the route.*

River Fowey below Respryn Bridge

Willy, 1,375ft high up on Bodmin Moor, is quite lovely here, and particularly so in spring and autumn. Follow the wooded path to reach double-railed Kathleen Bridge (1992), and cross the river. Follow the riverbank left; the path eventually bears right away from the river to pass through a red gate and meet a track **B**. *(The path to Restormel Castle goes off left here, through another red gate; walk across the fields to join a tarmac lane; where that lane bears right keep straight on along the farm lane to reach the castle, positioned on a high spur of land above the lane to the right.)*

Walk straight ahead up the track through woodland, slightly uphill, keeping left at the next fork of tracks.

Where the track bends 90° right turn left through a gate **C** and follow a track with fields right and woodland left. As you climb to enter Maudlin Wood through granite gateposts look out for the disused Jacob's quarry in the trees on the right. Stay on the track to meet another, where you turn sharp right under a huge oak tree **D**.

Follow the track through beech woodland steeply uphill. It levels (wonderful blackberries in autumn), with fields right and lovely views over the wooded Fowey Valley. The track passes through another dark red gate, then past Garden Cottage with its impressive walled garden (great hollyhocks in summer). Follow the gritty track on to pass through

If you do feel like exploring a little farther, it's worth going to visit the imposing ruins of **Restormel Castle**, refurbished by Edmund, Earl of Cornwall (1272–99), in the 13th century. Restormel, the best preserved motte-and-bailey castle in the county, was probably Edmund's main residence and, with its surrounding deer park, became a forceful symbol of Norman power and prosperity.

Lanhydrock's famous woodland garden, renowned for its camellias, rhododendrons and magnolias. The track ends at a wooden paling gateway **E**.

Go through the gate (note entrance to toilets, restaurant and shop left) and turn right along the wall of the formal gardens to reach the gatehouse. Turn right down The Avenue, flanked by a splendid double row of beech trees, to walk through glorious parkland to Newton Lodge; pass through the gates and walk straight on to meet the lane opposite Station Lodge. Turn right, and the National Trust car park will soon be found on the left.

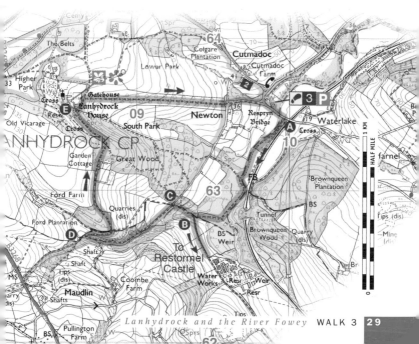

St Catherine's Castle

- Daymark
- sandy coves
- coast path
- historic sea port

The views over Fowey and Polruan, and up the Fowey River from St Catherine's Castle (a coastal fort), situated high above the sea on St Catherine's Head, have to be seen to be believed. This varied walk follows the coast path past secluded sandy coves to reach the 16th-century fort, which was built to protect the river-mouth from possible French attack.

St Catherine's Castle

walk 4

START Coombe car park, south west of Fowey

DISTANCE 2½ miles (4km)

TIME 1½ hours

PARKING National Trust car park at Coombe Farm (honesty box)

ROUTE FEATURES Some long ascents on coast path, several stiles (not all dog-friendly); track from car park to **A** very muddy after wet weather; dogs on leads through farmland

GPS WAYPOINTS
SX 109 511
A SX 107 509
B SX 104 505
C SX 118 509
D SX 117 509

PUBLIC TRANSPORT None available

REFRESHMENTS Cream teas at Coombe Farm in season; wide range of pubs and cafés in Fowey

PUBLIC TOILETS None en route; at Readymoney Cove

PLAY AREA None

ORDNANCE SURVEY MAPS Explorer 107 (St Austell & Liskeard), Landranger 200 (Newquay & Bodmin)

Walk through the gate in the top right corner of the car park and turn left down a green lane towards the coast. Follow this level track, which bends sharp right to end at a wooden gate into a field **A**.

Once through the gate turn left and walk around the edge of the field, following the hedge. There are good views ahead of the 84ft red-and-white striped daymark on Gribbin Head, built in 1832 as a navigational aid. Walk downhill to leave the field via a small

> **St Catherine's Castle** is managed by English Heritage, and is open all year round. It is a two-storey artillery fort, built in 1510, and later incorporated in Henry VIII's south coast defence system. This included larger castles at St Mawes and Pendennis Castle at Falmouth, both of which were built to protect the Fal Estuary, at that time the busiest port on the south coast. St Catherine's Castle was manned during the Civil War, refortified in the mid-19th century, and had anti-aircraft guns positioned there during the Second World War to protect craft massing in the estuary before the D-Day invasion on June 6, 1944.

wooden gate onto a narrow track. This runs downhill under trees and eventually through another gate to reach the coast path at secluded Polridmouth Cove **B**, a great place for a spot of rock-pooling. The pretty house overlooking the ornamental lake is on the site

Polruan from Fowey

of the old manorial corn mill for Menabilly, just inland, where the novelist Daphne Du Maurier lived for many years. Fowey celebrates her love of Cornwall by hosting the Daphne Du Maurier Festival of Arts & Literature every year in May.

Turn left along the coast path to gain Lankelly Cliff up a flight of wooden steps and over a stile. Walk along the edge of the field, then climb up the next hill to pass through an open gateway, with views of Polruan opening up ahead. The path drops to a small cove and over a stile, then runs along the next field edge. Pass through a gate and descend over a stepped bank to reach Coombe Haven. From there, ascend steeply uphill and over a stile to enter Allday's Fields. Pass through a small wooded gate into Covington Wood; follow the coast path right and onto St Catherine's Point; look carefully at the opposite headland to see the ruins of St Saviour's Chapel. Follow the path as it bears left, then turn right for the castle entrance **C**. There are wonderful views over Readymoney Cove, Fowey and upriver from here.

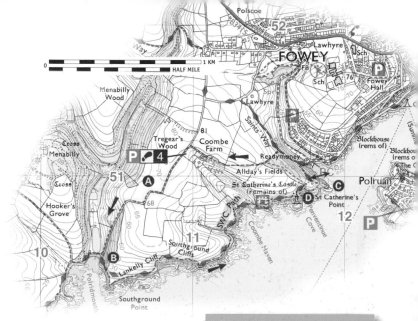

The church of **St Fimbarrus** in Fowey marks the end of the Saint's Way (Forth an Syns in Cornish), a 30-mile path that runs from the south door of Padstow parish church, on the north Cornish coast, and was conceived in 1984. It is thought to follow, in part at least, the line of an ancient cross-county route that linked a number of important religious sites.

? When were Allday's Fields given to the people of Fowey, and by whom?

Fowey took over from Lostwithiel as the main seaport for the area in the late 14th century, but in turn was superseded by Truro by the 15th. It is still a major port for the export of china clay, and the river buzzes with all kinds of maritime activity.

Retrace your steps into Allday's Fields, and bear right **D** uphill, keeping to the right of two seats. The path passes through an open gateway; walk diagonally left across the next field, keeping to the right of another seat, and go through a gate onto a track to pass Coombe Farm (left); continue up the lane to reach the car park on the left. ■

Cotehele

- Cotehele House
- old limekilns
- towering viaduct
- chapel in the wood

The historic village of Calstock, tucked away beside the tranquil River Tamar and now a mecca for local artists, provides a fitting start for a gentle riverside stroll which leads through woodland to beautiful Cotehele House, dating from the 15th/16th centuries, and its sympathetically restored quay, once a bustling port and lifeline for the Tamar Valley.

walk 5

Cotehele House

START Calstock

DISTANCE $3\frac{1}{2}$ miles (5.6km)

TIME $1\frac{1}{2}$ hours

PARKING Car park (free) in
Calstock

ROUTE FEATURES Fairly
steep path up through
woods from Cotehele
Quay; dogs are not allowed
within Cotehele garden

GPS WAYPOINTS

SX 436 685

Ⓐ SX 435 686

Ⓑ SX 425 690

Ⓒ SX 424 687

Ⓓ SX 423 685

Ⓔ SX 423 681

PUBLIC TRANSPORT Coach
service from Callington,
Tavistock via Gunnislake;
train from Plymouth/
Gunnislake

REFRESHMENTS National
Trust restaurant at
Cotehele (mid-Feb to
Christmas); NT tearoom
(mid-Feb to end Oct), picnic
area at Cotehele Quay;
The Tamar Inn, Calstock

PUBLIC TOILETS By the car
park in Calstock; at Cotehele

PLAY AREA By the car park
in Calstock; at Cotehele

ORDNANCE SURVEY MAPS
Explorer 108 (Lower Tamar
Valley & Plymouth),
Landranger 201 (Plymouth
& Launceston)

The last working sailing barge on the
Tamar, *Shamrock,* has been restored
and can be seen at Lime Quay. Built in 1899,
she is one of the country's last ketch-rigged
sailing barges; she originally carried manure
and traditional materials, and worked in the
stone trade around Truro and Falmouth for
many years. She is owned by the National
Trust and the National Maritime Museum.

From the car park walk towards the
river and turn right towards the elegant
12-arched viaduct over the Tamar, passing
The Tamar Inn (right). The viaduct was
built from 1904–8 to carry the railway
line from Calstock to Bere Alston. It's a
magnificent sight, soaring $117\frac{1}{2}$ ft above
the river, and dwarfing the picturesque
village of Calstock beneath. Follow the
lane round the pub to meet a junction;
turn left uphill (Commercial Road) Ⓐ.

Almost immediately, turn left along
Lower Kelly, a narrow lane that runs
along the edge of the river and passes
under the viaduct. Ahead and left you
can catch glimpses of Cotehele House
peering out from the trees. The lane
passes Calstock boatyard on the left and
a limekiln right, then runs under a bridge
and by another huge limekiln. Bear right
up the Danescombe Valley to pass the
pottery.

Where the track goes straight on, turn left **B** following signs for Cotehele to enter woodland. The path climbs steeply to reach a fork **C**.

Keep right, following signs for Cotehele House. Look left to see the 15th-century domed dovecote; the path reaches the track that separates the house from the lower gardens. Turn left, and walk on to pass through a gate with toilets, picnic area and 15th-century Barn Restaurant on the right. Keep ahead and then bear right past the entrance to the house and gardens.

Cotehele is a most beautifully preserved and atmospheric Tudor house, built largely between 1485 and 1539 by the Edgcumbe family. Owned by the National Trust since 1947, Cotehele is still a working estate, in much the same way as it has been for more than 600 years, with market gardening, flower growing and small-scale farming predominant. The varied gardens are superb all year round, and the valley garden that runs below the house downhill towards the Tamar provides an ideal location for a variety of tender and exotic species.

Where was the green lamppost outside Wood Cottage made, and by whom?

On reaching the lane **D** turn left downhill to 19th-century Cotehele Quay, with its beautifully restored warehouses and limekilns. The Higher (Lime) Quay was used for importing limestone (the oldest trade in the valley) to feed the kilns that can be seen all along the river, to produce calcium vital to correct the balance of the local acid soil; the Middle Quay brought in coal from South Wales; and the Lower Quay was used by paddle steamer passengers and for the export of the soft fruit and vegetables that were grown in the temperate climate of the Tamar Valley. Silver, lead, copper and arsenic were also mined in the valley from as early as the 14th century, until the 19th century, and exported from quays such as Cotehele, and Morwellham, near Tavistock.

Turn left to pass the Edgcumbe Arms tearoom **E** (a pub in the mid-19th century) and limekiln on the left, and the car park and picnic area right, and up onto a level path, which hits a broader track running along the edge of the woodland. The path climbs a little to pass the Chapel in the Wood, dedicated to

Culstock from Cotehele

St George and St Thomas à Becket, and built by Sir Richard Edgcumbe in 1490 in gratitude for his escape from his enemies in 1483. Continue along the path to pass the Calstock viewpoint high above the river on the right, and to rejoin the outward route **C**. Follow the path down through the woods; turn right by the pottery in Danescombe Valley, then retrace your steps along the banks of the Tamar to Calstock and your car. ■

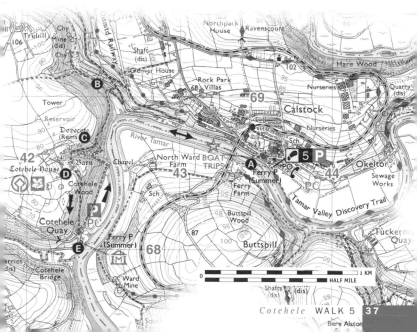

Trelissick

- **Riverside path**
- **superb views**
- **King Harry ferry**
- **parkland and gardens**

Starting from the National Trust's beautiful gardens at Trelissick, this gentle walk runs through mature parkland, then along the wooded Fal Estuary to the King Harry Ferry. Turning inland to follow a peaceful woodland path overlooking picturesque Lamouth Creek, the route climbs up to re-enter the Trelissick estate at the Old Lodge.

walk 6

View across Channals Creek

walk **6**

START Trelissick Garden

DISTANCE 3½ miles (5.6km)

TIME 1½ hours

PARKING National Trust car park at Trelissick Garden (free for members)

ROUTE FEATURES Well-surfaced paths throughout; big steps up from King Harry Ferry; steep ascent from **D** to **E**; dogs to be kept on leads in park

GPS WAYPOINTS

🥾 SW 835 396
Ⓐ SW 835 395
Ⓑ SW 836 391
Ⓒ SW 839 396
Ⓓ SW 831 400
Ⓔ SW 831 398

PUBLIC TRANSPORT Bus service from Truro

REFRESHMENTS Café at Trelissick (February – Christmas); icecream kiosk in car park (seasonal); Punchbowl & Ladle pub in Penelewey (north west of Trelissick); picnic area near car park

PUBLIC TOILETS Opposite NT shop at Trelissick

PLAY AREA None

ORDNANCE SURVEY MAPS Explorer 105 (Falmouth & Mevagissey), Landranger 204 (Truro & Falmouth)

Whether you park in the lower or higher car park, make for the information point by the icecream kiosk. Take the broad tarmac path signed Woodland Walk, soon passing through a small gate by the cattle-grid to enter the park, with lovely views down the Fal Estuary – also known as the Carrick Roads (from 'caryk rood', rocky harbour) – the third-largest natural harbour in the world.

Cross the drive that leads to the house **A**, and bear half left to walk across the open parkland towards the left side of Channals Creek, where there is access to the beach *(note that the land immediately behind the sea wall is very wet, so it's best to keep bearing left to avoid that)*. Wherever you meet the sea wall, turn left and keep ahead to reach a kissing-gate. The park was laid out in the

Trelissick House was built around 1750, and sold in 1805 to mining entrepreneur Ralph Daniel. In the early 19th century his son Thomas laid out the extensive carriage drives that run through the estate. The Gilbert family took over in 1844 and further developed the house, but the beautiful gardens were largely created by Leonard Cunliffe, his stepdaughter Ida Copeland, and her husband Ronald. The gardens are famous for their tender exotic plants, encouraged by their sheltered position and mild climate. The 376-acre estate was given to the National Trust in 1955.

mid-18th century to complement the first house, built by John Lawrence, which has since been extended, and is not open to the public.

Pass through the kissing-gate  and follow the narrow, gritty path under twisted oak and sweet chestnut trees along the edge of the River Fal. This lovely, level path leads through South Wood, and has the added interest of

The Tower at Trelissick

all kinds of vessels passing by on the water. The path broadens as it passes below Trelissick Garden and meets a junction (ignore the right turn signed 'Ferry' as this leads to the passenger ferry across the Fal). Bear left to meet the road **C**. To take a look at the King Harry Ferry turn right downhill. The ferry began operating in 1888 and links the west side of the Fal with the Roseland Peninsula. The original ferry saw service from 1889 until 1913; the present ferry – the seventh – began operations in May 2006. The ferry saves an amazing 4.5 million car miles every year.

> ✳ The remains of an Iron Age fort have been found above **Roundwood Quay** (which can be seen across Lamouth Creek), the earliest evidence of prehistoric settlement here, and probably built to control the upper reaches of the Fal. The 18th-century wharves at the quay were used for shipping out tin and copper, which was smelted and refined on site, and in the mid-19th century the quay was still the scene of some activity, with a malt house, lime kiln and shipbuilding.

> ❓ *How often does the King Harry ferry run?*

Retrace your steps to **C**, and turn right up steps into North Wood. The

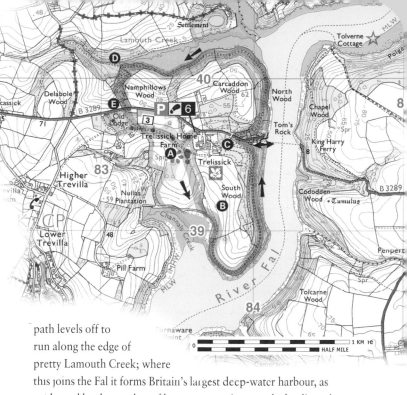

path levels off to
run along the edge of
pretty Lamouth Creek; where
this joins the Fal it forms Britain's largest deep-water harbour, as
evidenced by the number of huge ocean-going vessels that lie up here,
and which add an unexpected element to this route. Follow the path to a
junction **D**, with Roundwood fort and quay signed ahead and right.

Turn left, away from the creek, signed Trelissick. The path zigzags very
steeply uphill to reach the road at a wooden gate **E**.

Cross the road with care to re-enter the Trelissick parkland by the early
19th-century neo-Grecian Old Lodge, and walk straight on through Old
Lodge beech plantation. The path bears left and downhill to meet the
drive to the house. Turn left through a wooden gate by the cattle-grid
and follow the drive through open parkland, which has a wonderfully
informal and relaxing feel. At the fork bear left back to the starting point
of the walk and the car park. ∎

Tintagel

- **Ancient cliff castle**
- **stunning views**
- **coast path**
- **old chapel**

walk 7

It's not hard to get carried away with romantic notions as you gaze over the ruins of Tintagel Castle, magnificently situated on the north Cornish coast, where tales of King Arthur abound. Our route leads along the coast path to the castle entrance, then runs around craggy Barras Nose, with glorious views all around, before returning via Tintagel village.

Looking over Tintagel Haven from Barras Nose

walk 7

START St Materiana's Church

DISTANCE 3 miles (4.8km)

TIME 1½ hours

PARKING Parking area (free) by St Materiana's Church, signposted from centre of village

ROUTE FEATURES Coast path rocky and undulating; steep descent to Tintagel Haven; field paths sometimes muddy; dogs on leads through farmland; non-dog-friendly stiles

GPS WAYPOINTS

- SX 050 884
- **A** SX 051 888
- **B** SX 051 890
- **C** SX 053 893
- **D** SX 059 891
- **E** SX 056 888

PUBLIC TRANSPORT Bus service from Camelford via Wadebridge, St Columb Major, Bude (to Tintagel village)

REFRESHMENTS Castle Beach Café (open all year) at castle entrance; wide range of pubs and cafés in Tintagel

PUBLIC TOILETS At castle entrance; in Tintagel village

PLAY AREA None

ORDNANCE SURVEY MAPS Explorer 111 (Bude, Boscastle & Tintagel), Landranger 200 (Newquay & Bodmin)

From the car park walk right along the well-marked coast path, passing St Materiana's Church on the right. Almost immediately, views of the flat-topped island on which part of the castle is built, rising 250ft above the sea, open up ahead and left. The path drops down a flight of uneven steps and through a break in the hedgebank to leave Glebe Cliff by an NT contributions cairn **A**.

Follow the cliff-edge wall downhill to reach the upper entrance to the castle (under the care of English Heritage), then follow coast path signs right and sharp left to zigzag down to reach the main track to the castle, with the public toilets on the left. Turn left to pass the English Heritage shop on the left, and the café across the stream on the right, to reach the sea at Tintagel Haven **B**, from where you can gaze in awe at the

> **St Materiana** has been identified with St Madryn, a Welsh princess said to have been active in this part of Cornwall around AD 500. The 12th-century church, set in splendid isolation on Glebe Cliff, is thought to have been built on the site of an oratory which was linked to her main shrine at Minster, a few miles inland. The discovery of 5th-century slate-lined graves at the church indicate that this could have been a burial site for important people, presumably from the castle.

ruined walls and buildings on the island towering above you. Most of the visible ruins date from the 13th-century, when Richard, Earl of Cornwall, carried out a massive refortification of this naturally defensive site. There is evidence of Celtic occupation here too, and it is likely that Tintagel was occupied by someone of great importance until the 8th century, when it was abandoned.

For generations **Tintagel** has been linked with legends of King Arthur and the Knights of the Round Table. It is easy to understand why when you visit the castle and let your imagination wander: it's a wonderfully evocative place. Although several sites share the claim, many believe that Arthur was born here. He is most likely to have been a powerful warrior famed for his battles against Saxon invaders.

Turn right to cross the stream on a footbridge, then up steep steps, following coast path signs uphill to pass wooden railings. Pass a National Trust sign indicating that you have reached Barras Nose, then follow the path downhill over a footbridge. Take the path leading left to reach the end of the Barras Nose headland **C**, with wonderful views of the castle to the left, and towards the next headland, Willapark, to the right.

Walk inland to rejoin the coast path and turn left to pass a coast path sign to Bossiney. The coast path runs through a gate and along Smith's Cliff, then bears inland to meet a grassy area **D**.

At a footpath post (coast path left) turn right uphill, keeping the hedgebank left. At the top go through a gate and along the left edge of the field; cross a stream on stone slabs (wet in winter). Leave that field over a stone slab stile onto a hedged farm drive, which meets a tarmac lane by The Headland camping and caravanning park (left) **E**.

Walk straight on along the lane through busy Tintagel village, which is best negotiated quickly and can be a shock after the majesty of the castle and coastline. The lane curves sharp left to pass the track to the castle (right); turn right down the next lane, signposted to parish church/Glebe Cliff. At the bottom of the hill look out for the tiny 13th/14th-century Chapel of Our Lady of Fontevrault, built into the vicarage gatehouse. Continue up the lane, keeping ahead through the churchyard, and back to your car. ■

St Materiana's Church

? When was the Barras Nose purchased by the National trust, and why?

St Agnes

- Tin-mining remains
- sea views
- stunning coastline
- St Agnes Beacon

A glimpse into Cornwall's industrial past can be gained on this lovely route that leads along the magnificent cliffs around St Agnes Head to pass Wheal Coates, now National Trust, before ascending St Agnes Beacon. On a clear day the views all over north Cornwall from the top of the beacon are superb – and in late summer the cliffs and beacon glow purple under a carpet of heather.

View towards Wheal Coates

walk 8

START Carn Gowla

DISTANCE 3½ miles (5.6km)

TIME 1½ hours

PARKING Car park (free) at Carn Gowla, just south of St Agnes Head

ROUTE FEATURES Track from **F** to **G** muddy in winter; many paths crossing St Agnes Beacon; dogs to be kept under control at all times

GPS WAYPOINTS
- 🥾 SW 699 512
- **A** SW 698 503
- **B** SW 698 500
- **C** SW 700 500
- **D** SW 708 499
- **E** SW 710 502
- **F** SW 707 508
- **G** SW 704 516

PUBLIC TRANSPORT Bus service from Perranporth and Truro to St Agnes village only

REFRESHMENTS None on route; picnic area near St Agnes Head; wide range of pubs and cafés in St Agnes

PUBLIC TOILETS None en route

PLAY AREA None

ORDNANCE SURVEY MAPS Explorer 104 (Redruth & St Agnes), Landranger 203 (Land's End & Isles of Scilly)

🥾 From the parking area follow the coast path south past granite boulders on a gritty track that runs along the cliffs at Tubby's Head, with fantastic views towards the sandy beaches at Chapel Porth and Porthtowan, and beyond to Godrevy Point.

> ✱ Deep underground mining was carried out at **Wheal Coates** from the 1870s, concentrating on workings just below low-tide mark, and 138 people worked here in 1881. After various periods of closure and reopening, the mine finally ceased operation in 1914. The three largest buildings on the site are engine houses, and have been beautifully restored. The shaft from Towanroath is 600ft deep, and is (fortunately) protected by a grille today.

A Where the SWC Path rejoins the route, keep straight ahead on a level track to reach the restored buildings at Wheal Coates. Note the gashes and gulleys in the heather and gorse en route, evidence of medieval opencast mining when tin-bearing veins (lodes) were dug out. Take some time to explore Wheal Coates; you will learn a huge amount about the history of Cornish tin-mining here. For a good view of the impressive Towanroath engine house walk a little way along the cliff

? *How high is St Agnes Beacon?*

and look back towards the cliffs below Stamps engine house. Retrace your steps to the information board on Whim engine house.

B Turn right inland on a gritty path, soon passing a chimney. Follow the path past Wheal Coates car park to meet a lane **C**.

Turn left; a little way up the lane, turn right up the drive for Beacon Cottage Farm touring park between granite gateposts. Keep on the drive to pass the farmhouse; keep ahead through the farmyard and walk straight on eventually to meet three gateways ahead; go through the one on the left, as signed. Keeping the hedgebank left walk round the field edge, eventually crossing a stile onto the beacon. The area has long been a valuable source of very young sands and clays (under 50 million years); in times past clay was used to hold miners' candles when underground, securing them either on to rocks, or on to the miners' hats.

Stamps engine house

Walk ahead on a grassy path, which bears left **D** and climbs to the beacon trig point **E**.

From the trig point walk ahead, taking the right of the two obvious paths running along the ridge. Ignoring all other paths follow the path as it bears left round the end of the hill and runs towards the coast. When the lane comes into view below right look for an obvious narrow path on the right; follow this down to the lane **F**.

Turn right along the lane and immediately left down a rough track; where it turns sharp right, go straight

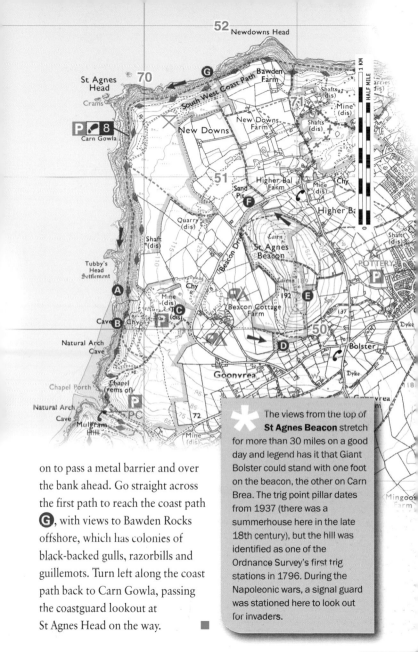

on to pass a metal barrier and over the bank ahead. Go straight across the first path to reach the coast path **G**, with views to Bawden Rocks offshore, which has colonies of black-backed gulls, razorbills and guillemots. Turn left along the coast path back to Carn Gowla, passing the coastguard lookout at St Agnes Head on the way. ∎

The views from the top of **St Agnes Beacon** stretch for more than 30 miles on a good day and legend has it that Giant Bolster could stand with one foot on the beacon, the other on Carn Brea. The trig point pillar dates from 1937 (there was a summerhouse here in the late 18th century), but the hill was identified as one of the Ordnance Survey's first trig stations in 1796. During the Napoleonic wars, a signal guard was stationed here to look out for invaders.

The Lizard to Church Cove

- Southernmost point
- coast path
- lifeboat station
- ancient church

walk 9

This refreshing walk, starting from mainland England's southernmost point, meanders along the cliff top, glorious with wildflowers in summer, past some fascinating features – the Lizard lighthouse, the chasm of the Lion's Den, Lloyd's signal station and the lifeboat station at Kilcobben Cove – before turning inland to return via the lovely church of St Wynwallow.

Lizard Point

walk 9

START The Lizard

DISTANCE $3\frac{1}{2}$ miles (5.6km)

TIME $1\frac{3}{4}$ hours

PARKING National Trust car park near lighthouse (NT members free)

ROUTE FEATURES High and uneven steps down to and up from Housel Bay; *steep ascent inland* from Church Cove; dogs to be kept under control at all times

GPS WAYPOINTS

🖉 SW 702 117
Ⓐ SW 702 115
Ⓑ SW 701 114
Ⓒ SW 715 120
Ⓓ SW 715 125
Ⓔ SW 714 127
Ⓕ SW 707 126

PUBLIC TRANSPORT Bus service from Truro via Helston

REFRESHMENTS Polpeor Café and Wave Crest Café at Lizard Point: cafés, fish and chips and Top House pub in Lizard village

PUBLIC TOILETS In car park and signposted off green in Lizard village

PLAY AREA Opposite Beacon Terrace, towards the end of the walk

ORDNANCE SURVEY MAPS Explorer 103 (The Lizard), Landranger 203 (Land's End & Isles of Scilly)

> ✳ The signal station at **Bass Point** was built in 1872 by shipping agents G.C. Fox & Co, and is further evidence of the strategic significance of the Lizard peninsula. More than 1,000 ships a month were using the station by 1878. Part of the building was leased to Lloyd's of London in 1883, to report the arrival of ships from across the Atlantic to London. Since 1992 it has been in the hands of the National Trust.

🖉 Walk towards the coast on a gritty path, to pass the toilets (left); select either the stepped or non-stepped path (as signed) and descend to join the coast path Ⓐ.

Turn right and walk along the path to find Lizard Point Ⓑ (visited by over 100,000 people every year) which, despite its famed position at 49° 57' N latitude, and 5° 12' W longitude, is something of a disappointment. But the coastal scenery is fantastic, and in the summer the cliffs glow yellow and magenta under a blanket of mysenbryanthemum (Hottentot fig). There are also a couple of interesting serpentine workshops here: some believe that the name 'Lizard' derives in part from the underlying rock of the peninsula which, when wet, resembles the skin of a snake. Look out, too, for the old lifeboat station in Polpeor Cove to the west, which ran from 1859 to 1961.

? *Who was lost at sea on the night of December 29, 1962?*

From Lizard Point retrace your steps along the coast path to pass the path back to the car park. The path runs below the lighthouse, built in 1752 to oversee one of the busiest shipping lanes in the world; it became automated in 1999. The path runs along the cliff to pass the Lion's Den to the right, formed in 1842 when the roof of a sea cave collapsed, and on to drop steeply down steps to the back of Housel Cove. Cross the stream on a concrete bridge, and follow the path up steps; at the next junction of paths turn right on the coast path to pass below the gardens of the the Housel Bay Hotel. Walk on towards Pen Olver, passing by the experimental Marconi wireless station, set up in 1900, and then past Lloyd's signal station and the voluntary National Coastwatch station on Bass Point. Keep on the coast path to pass a pink house and continue briefly along a track.

C Turn right and follow the coast path along the cliffs to Kilcobben Cove. Walk up the steps to reach the Lizard lifeboat station **D**.

Descend steps by the lifeboat station and follow the coast path to pretty Church Cove – formerly the site of a pilchard fishery – at a concrete walkway **E**.

Turn right to have a look at the cove, then walk straight up the walkway which runs steeply uphill past thatched cottages. The ancient church of St Wynwallow, with its squat serpentine tower, is passed on the right; there is thought to have been a church here since about AD 600, and parts of the existing building date to the 12th century,

✱ RNLI lifeboats were stationed at **Polpeor Cove** until 1961, and at **Cadgwith** from 1867–1963; there was also one for a brief time at Church Cove at the end of the 19th century. The new station at Kilcobben Cove was built in 1958 in a sheltered position from which launching can take place in any weather conditions.

followed by refurbishments in the 13th, 15th and 19th centuries. Situated in the parish of Landewednack, it is the most southerly place of worship in England. It was here that the last sermon in Cornish was delivered, in 1670. Follow the lane on; at the fork by The Forge, keep left on the main lane to reach a T-junction **F**.

Turn left to pass Cross Common Nursery on the right (with its impressive range of exotic plants). Opposite the school turn left over the hedgebank on stone steps, signed public footpath. Walk diagonally across the field, aiming for the corner of the playing field on the right, then turn right, keeping the hedgebank on the right. The path bears round the end of the field and through a kissing-gate. Pass the farm (left) on a gritty track to meet the lane. Cross the lane and follow the footpath, which runs parallel to the road and then crosses it to lead back to the car park. ■

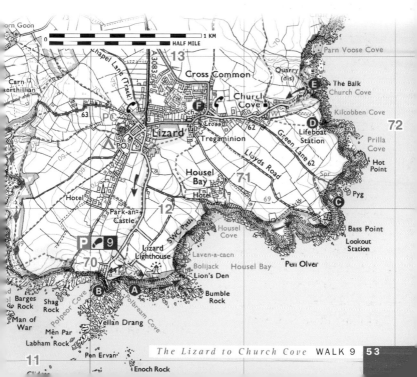

Veryan and Portloe

■ Old fishing village   ■ country lanes
■ roundhouses   ■ coast path

walk 10

Veryan is perhaps best known for its five roundhouses, seen on so many picture postcards. But just a mile or so away lies the coast and the old fishing village of Portloe, which makes an excellent focus for an easy walk through rolling farmland and quiet lanes – and there's even a pub at each end.

Portloe

walk 10

START Veryan

DISTANCE 3½ miles (5.6km)

TIME 1¾ hours

PARKING On the side of the road near the school in the village centre

ROUTE FEATURES Field paths muddy in winter; dogs on leads through farmland; *steep climb* out of Portloe to Sunny Corner; coast path narrow and exposed round Jacka Point

GPS WAYPOINTS
- ◢ SW 915 395
- Ⓐ SW 918 396
- Ⓑ SW 920 394
- Ⓒ SW 929 390
- Ⓓ SW 929 389
- Ⓔ SW 937 394
- Ⓕ SW 933 394
- Ⓖ SW 924 397

PUBLIC TRANSPORT Bus service from St Austell and Truro

REFRESHMENTS The New Inn and Ellerkey Coffee Shop, Veryan; Ship Inn and Lugger Hotel, Portloe; icecream March – November at The Roseland Nursery, Trewartha Chapel

PUBLIC TOILETS In the centre of Veryan; in Portloe

PLAY AREA At start

ORDNANCE SURVEY MAPS Explorer 105 (Falmouth & Mevagissey), Landranger 204 (Truro & Falmouth)

◢ Cross the road from the school to the footpath by the ornamental gardens, signed 'To Portloe via Trewartha'. Walk through the wooden gate and along the path, with the church above right. The path leads through a kissing-gate into the playground. Walk to the top right corner, cross the stream and into the field over a Cornish stile. Bear half right up the field, aiming for a stile on a hedge corner Ⓐ.

> Veryan's pretty church of **St Symphorian** (a French saint dating from the 13th century), largely rebuilt in 1847, is well worth investigation. In the churchyard can be found what is reputed to be the longest grave in Britain, holding the crew of the German barque *Hera*. She was wrecked on the Gull Rock in 1914, and the crew of 19 were buried in one long grave, paid for by the parish.

Turn right over the stile to enter a narrow strip of woodland. Keep ahead, uphill, eventually with a stream right. Leave the woodland via a stile, and walk along the right edge of the field. Pass through a gate in the top right corner (wet underfoot) to meet Century Lane Ⓑ.

Turn left. At the crossroads go straight ahead, signed Portloe. Pass Camels House on the left, with its unusual 'decorated' wall; look out for glimpses of the sea ahead. Eventually the lane bends sharp left **C**.

Keep ahead through the gates to Broome Parc, which was used in the TV adaptation of Mary Wesley's *The Camomile Lawn* in 1991. Follow the National Trust footpath between the house and the walled garden, to reach the coast path **D**.

The building of Veryan's famous **roundhouses** was initiated by the rector, and they were constructed by a builder from Lostwithiel around 1820. Each one is adorned with a cross, and the idea behind their shape is that the Devil would be unable to hide in a house with no corners. There is a pair of these pretty little buildings, with Gothic revival windows, at each end of the village, and one in the centre. Veryan also has two holy wells.

Turn sharp left by the coast path post and follow the path below the garden, edged with hydrangeas. Go up a steep flight of steps and over a hedgebank, then over a wooden stile into a field; look back for lovely views over Parc Caragloose Cove, and Nare Head and Gull Rock beyond. Continue along the coast path, and through a kissing-gate to reach a gorsey area above Manare Point, with views ahead to Dodman Point. Follow the coast path downhill towards the pretty, unspoilt fishing village of Portloe, situated at the mouth of a narrow valley. Keep right to follow the coast path around the edge of the jagged igneous outcrop of rock known as The Jacka (*watch out for areas of unfenced cliff*), then turns inland to reach the slipway **E**, with public toilets on the left. Portloe's little harbour was partly responsible for the fact that during the 17 years that a lifeboat was stationed here it never once saw action: in rough weather it was impossible to negotiate the narrow entrance.

From the slipway turn left uphill to pass the church (right). Go straight on, climbing steeply past The Ship Inn (right). When houses at Sunny Corner are reached, turn right **F** over the stream, signed public footpath to Veryan. Follow the tarmac drive to the left to pass in front of The Old White Cottage, and go through a small metal gate into a field.

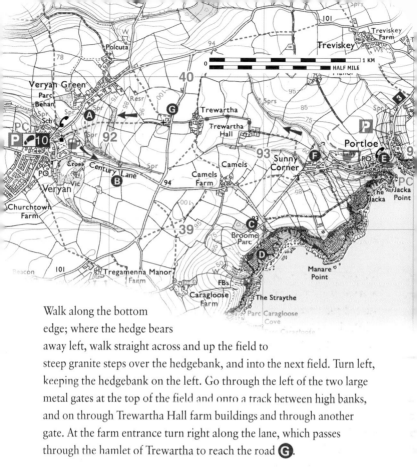

Walk along the bottom
edge; where the hedge bears
away left, walk straight across and up the field to
steep granite steps over the hedgebank, and into the next field. Turn left,
keeping the hedgebank on the left. Go through the left of the two large
metal gates at the top of the field and onto a track between high banks,
and on through Trewartha Hall farm buildings and through another
gate. At the farm entrance turn right along the lane, which passes
through the hamlet of Trewartha to reach the road **G**.

Turn left then, almost immediately, right on a lane, signed Veryan,
to pass the converted Trewartha Chapel and The Roseland Nursery.
The lane ends at a gate into a field; walk straight across the field and
through a narrow strip of woodland via two hedgebanks and a gate.
Walk half left downhill to
meet the outward route at **A**.
Retrace your steps back
through the playground to
your car. ■

> **?** *Who was responsible
> for erecting the well in
> Veryan, which you can find
> near the public toilets?*

Porthcurno and Treen

- ■ Cliff theatre
- ■ sandy beaches
- ■ stunning views
- ■ cliff castle

walk 11

The white sands and turquoise sea at Porthcurno draw hundreds of holidaymakers on a sunny day. But it is easy to escape the crowds and explore the beautiful coastline around the cove, including the remarkable and superbly situated Minack Theatre, and craggy Logan Rock with Treryn Dinas Iron Age fort, perched high above the waves.

Porthcurno beach, looking towards Logan Rock

walk 11

START Porthcurno

DISTANCE $3\frac{1}{2}$ miles (5.6km)

TIME $1\frac{3}{4}$ hours

PARKING Car park (fee-paying) at Porthcurno beach

ROUTE FEATURES Steep walk up lane to Minack; high uneven steps down towards beach; narrow and exposed path along Treen Cliff; dogs to be kept under control at all times

GPS WAYPOINTS
- ✏ SW 384 225
- Ⓐ SW 384 222
- Ⓑ SW 386 223
- Ⓒ SW 393 225
- Ⓓ SW 397 223
- Ⓔ SW 394 231
- Ⓕ SW 387 230

PUBLIC TRANSPORT Bus service from Land's End and Penzance

REFRESHMENTS The Porthcurno Beach café and Cable Station Inn at Porthcurno; café and Logan Rock pub in Treen; café at Minack Theatre

PUBLIC TOILETS In Porthcurno car park and by the café in Treen

PLAY AREA None

ORDNANCE SURVEY MAPS Explorer 102 (Land's End), Landranger 203 (Land's End & Isles of Scilly)

✱ Just above the main car park can be found another of this sheltered spot's surprises, **Porthcurno Telegraph Museum**. Porthcurno was first used for communication purposes in the 1870s, from which time undersea cables were brought here from all over the world. For more than 90 years it was one of the most important centres for communication in the country. During the Second World War it played a vital role as a secret communications centre.

👣 From the car park walk left on the lane, which climbs steeply uphill to reach the entrance to the Minack Theatre on the left Ⓐ.

Turn left towards the theatre, and walk through the car park to the entrance. Follow the coast path to the left of the entrance down big, rugged steps round the edge of the theatre, with glorious views over the beach and clear water – on a hot sunny day you could be somewhere in the Mediterranean. The Minack Theatre is the result of one woman's inspiration and determination: Rowena Cade (1893–1983), who originated from Cheltenham, and who started cutting out the theatre site by hand in 1932. This wonderful place now puts on a 17-week

❓ *When was the Eastern Telegraph Company formed?*

summer season of plays, come rain or shine. It has a visitor centre and museum, café and gift shop, and a superb display of sub-tropical plants. Follow the path inland then across the back of the beach to a path junction **B**.

Follow the coast path up the other side of the beach – it's a bit of a scramble – to reach a pillbox. At the next junction of paths turn right. At the next coast path post turn right to leave the coast path on a narrow path that runs along the cliff edge to reach a white pyramid, marking the site of the wooden hut that housed the end of the submarine telegraph cable laid from Brest in 1880. Follow the narrow path along the cliff edge as it runs behind Treen Cove to rejoin the coast path **C**.

Turn right onto Treen Cliff; ignore the bridlepath leading left, and take either of the two paths ahead – they soon join up.

At an old NT contributions cairn **D**, bear right to walk out onto the headland to have a look at the Logan Rock. This is also the site of Treryn Dinas, an Iron Age cliff castle, perched high above the weathered granite cliffs. The *Granite State* was wrecked off the Logan Rock in 1898.

Retrace your steps to **D**, and go straight ahead inland through the fields. Cross over two Cornish stiles, then over stone steps across the next hedgebank, and through a gap in the next bank. The path ends at a kissing-gate; turn left along the rough track towards Treen. Where the track bends left, go straight ahead over

> ✳ A logan stone is a rocking stone, and the **Logan Rock** here is famous for being dislodged from its position in 1824 by naval **Lieutenant Goldsmith** and his friends, causing a public outcry. He was ordered to replace it by the Admiralty at his own expense, a complicated procedure considering the granite rock weighs more than 60 tons. It can still be rocked, but not as easily as in Lieutenant Goldsmith's time. Guides to the Logan Rock used to pick sea pinks from the cliffs for sale, and so became known as 'pinkers'.

granite steps to meet the lane by Larks Cottage; turn right for the Logan café and stores, toilets and car park. Bear left down the lane to find the Logan Inn **E**, which has a great collection of old black-and-white photographs that detail the escapades of Lieutenant Goldsmith.

Retrace your steps from the pub back up the lane. Where the lane bears left towards the café keep ahead, then bear right as signed on a footpath. Cross a Cornish stile and keep up the left edge of two fields, then across the next. Keep ahead to cross four more stiles to reach Trendrennen Farm. Turn left towards a stile, but do not cross it; instead bear left again to find a small gate marked with a blue arrow **F**.

Keep ahead down the narrow walled path (wet in places), eventually to meet the coast path. Turn right and follow a narrow path straight ahead downhill (leaving the coast path again) to meet a track. Turn right for the car park. ∎

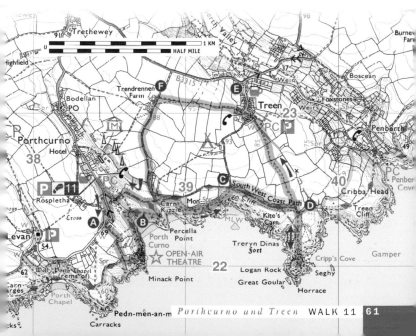

Geevor and Levant

■ **Lighthouse** ■ **restored beam engine**
■ **tin-mining remains** ■ **mining villages**

walk 12

Every visitor to Cornwall should take some time to learn about the county's past, and in this remote and sometimes desolate part of West Penwith there is plenty of evidence of her industrial heritage, stamped on a stunning natural coastline. The walk leads through the fascinating remains of the Geevor and Levant tin mines, now partly restored and open to the public.

Levant mine

walk **12**

START Pendeen lighthouse

DISTANCE 4 miles (6.4km)

TIME 1¾ hours

PARKING Pendeen Lighthouse, signposted from the B3306 in Pendeen

ROUTE FEATURES Undulating coast path from Pendeen Lighthouse to Geevor, very muddy in places in winter; dogs to be kept under control at all times

GPS WAYPOINTS

- ✏ SW 379 358
- Ⓐ SW 380 354
- Ⓑ SW 372 347
- Ⓒ SW 367 344
- Ⓓ SW 373 338
- Ⓔ SW 374 344

PUBLIC TRANSPORT Bus service from St Ives, and from Penzance via St Just (to Pendeen)

REFRESHMENTS Count House Café at Geevor

PUBLIC TOILETS At Geevor

PLAY AREA None

ORDNANCE SURVEY MAPS Explorer 102 (Land's End), Landranger 203 (Land's End & Isles of Scilly)

✱ The **Levant** mine closed in 1930, and its workings are now flooded by the sea. Take some time to have a look at Levant's indoor beam engine, the oldest surviving example in Cornwall. It was built by Harvey's of Hayle and has been restored by the Trevithick Society. Owned by the National Trust, there are regular steaming days throughout the year. The Levant mining disaster exhibition also offers a dramatic insight into the hardships and dangers of this 2,000-year-old industry.

👢 From Pendeen Lighthouse walk along the lane inland to reach the coastguard cottages on the left. The lighthouse was built in 1900 to augment the Longships and Trevose lighthouses, views of which could be obscured by high cliffs from certain angles. The lighthouse, run by the Trevithick Trust, is sometimes open to the public. It holds the largest surviving siren fog signal in Britain. It was automated in 1995.

Opposite cottage No 6 Ⓐ turn right by the granite marker signed Cape Cornwall; follow the coast path downhill to cross a stream. Walk up onto Boscaswell Cliff and through a gate to reach Carn Ros; look ahead for good views of the Victorian settling tanks, chimneys and buildings connected with the old tin mines at Trewellard Bottoms. The greenish stain on the cliffs ahead indicates the presence of copper. Follow the coast path

Pendeen Lighthouse

signs to cross a wooden bridge and round the back of the cove, then uphill to reach a footpath post and entrance to Geevor **B**.

Keep ahead on the coast path, signed Levant. Keep going to reach the car park for Levant, with the mine and beam engine on the cliffs right.

C Turn left and walk inland up the lane to reach the edge of Trewellard, passing the ruins of Higher Bal mine on the way.

Just past the 30mph sign turn left by Pentrew **D**. Follow the lane straight on to pass Merrivale House (left). Keep straight on to pass through farm buildings; the lane becomes a track, then reduces to a narrow path between low walls. Follow this downhill; look right towards the old mine buildings at Geevor Tin Mine Heritage Centre. Most of these date from the 20th century, and now house the museum (restored and revitalised in 2008), café and

? *Why is the Mexico shaft at Geevor so named?*

shop. You can also visit the late 19th-century carpenter's shop and stables, and the 1850s count house (the original mine offices).

When level with the café and shop turn right over a stile **E**, and then another. Turn left as signed (Levant) and cross a stile in the fence, with

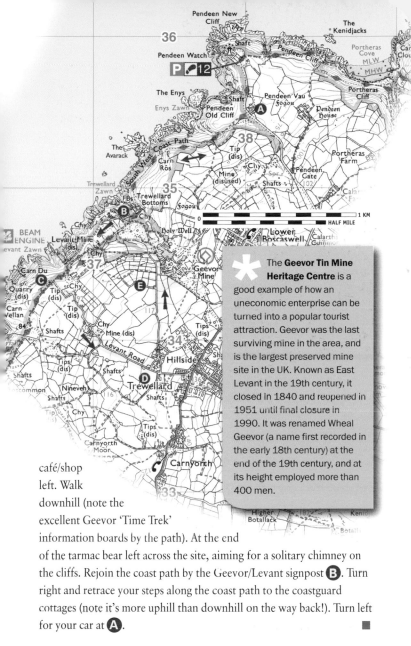

The **Geevor Tin Mine Heritage Centre** is a good example of how an uneconomic enterprise can be turned into a popular tourist attraction. Geevor was the last surviving mine in the area, and is the largest preserved mine site in the UK. Known as East Levant in the 19th century, it closed in 1840 and reopened in 1951 until final closure in 1990. It was renamed Wheal Geevor (a name first recorded in the early 18th century) at the end of the 19th century, and at its height employed more than 400 men.

café/shop left. Walk downhill (note the excellent Geevor 'Time Trek' information boards by the path). At the end of the tarmac bear left across the site, aiming for a solitary chimney on the cliffs. Rejoin the coast path by the Geevor/Levant signpost **B**. Turn right and retrace your steps along the coast path to the coastguard cottages (note it's more uphill than downhill on the way back!). Turn left for your car at **A**.

■

Coverack

- ■ **Old fishing village**
- ■ **raised beach**
- ■ **working quarry**
- ■ **delicious icecream**

walk 13

A walk along the coast path as it runs north-east from the picturesque old fishing village of Coverack is quite a surprise, as the coast here is low-lying and somewhat 'un-Cornish' in character. The walk passes a working quarry, then runs inland along quiet lanes to reach the delights of Roskilly's icecream at Tregellast Barton – definitely worth the effort of getting there.

Towards Lowland Point

walk 13

START Coverack

DISTANCE 5 miles (8km)

TIME 3 hours

PARKING St Keverne parish council charity car park (honesty box); also car park (fee-paying) above

ROUTE FEATURES Parts of coast path wet and boggy all year round; *demanding climb inland from* **C**; dogs to be kept under control at all times

GPS WAYPOINTS

  📌 SW 782 185

  A SW 799 194

  B SW 802 199

  C SW 799 204

  D SW 794 208

  E SW 792 205

  F SW 789 199

PUBLIC TRANSPORT Bus service from Truro via Helston

REFRESHMENTS The Paris Hotel and The Wave café in Coverack; Croust House restaurant and café at Roskilly's; occasional picnic tables near Dean quarries, and in Countryside Stewardship land near Roskilly's

PUBLIC TOILETS In the car park; at Roskilly's

PLAY AREA At start

ORDNANCE SURVEY MAPS Explorer 103 (The Lizard), Landranger 203 (Land's End & Isles of Scilly)

👣 Walk downhill from the car park towards the sea.

Turn left along the tarmac lane signed coast path. The lane becomes a gritty track and ends at a five-bar gate; turn right down the narrow coast path through trees and onto open low cliffs. The coast path runs over a series of banks, stiles, stepping stones and grassy areas, and is often wet.

Eventually cross a stile onto National Trust land at Lowland Point **A**, a raised beach dating from an interglacial period within the last Ice Age when the sea level was higher. The steep hill inland was the original cliff. Lowland Point also has

> ✳ The old fishing village of **Coverack** had a thriving pilchard fishing fleet from medieval times to the early years of the 20th century, and also a fairly healthy reputation for smuggling. A lifeboat was stationed here until 1963, largely on account of **The Manacles** (see panel on next page).
>
> The rather grand-sounding Paris Hotel is named after the *Paris*, which was stranded off the coast in 1899.

evidence of prehistoric occupation in the form of field boundaries and hut remains. Follow the coast path on to cross a stile into Dean quarries, where gabbro – an igneous rock used widely as roadstone and in coastal defence building – is mined (there's a picnic table a few steps beyond the stile). On the far side of the quarries lies Godrevy Cove, from where the notorious Long Meadow Gang of smugglers operated in the 18th century.

> ? *When does blasting take place at Dean quarries, and how would you know it was going to happen?*

A noticeboard **B** gives details of blasting and warning signals (to see one of the disused quarries follow the coast path for 100 yds to a viewing area on the left). From the board turn left inland and climb steeply up the edge of a huge tip: the upper part of the path (partly stepped) has a handrail. Pass a picnic table at the top and keep along the path, which bears right and through a gate, then bears left to meet the drive at Treglohan **C**.

* The craggy rocks visible off Lowland Point are the infamous **Manacles**, particularly dangerous to shipping as they are almost submerged at high tide. Before radar was invented, ships tended to hug the coast, and The Manacles have claimed many victims over the centuries, including the *John*, wrecked in 1855 en route from Plymouth to Canada, with the loss of 196 lives. In 1898 the *Mohegan* foundered on the rocks, and more than 100 passengers and crew lie buried in St Keverne church-yard. Interestingly. St Keverne's Church tower is a mix of tower and spire, with the intention of creating a very obvious landmark to warn mariners away from The Manacles.

Turn right down the drive (note picnic table right) to meet the lane, and turn left. Follow the lane past Trythance, then cut out a lane kink by crossing a stile and field corner, then another stile. Meet a staggered crossroads of lanes **D** (note the Countryside Stewardship area on the right: ponds, woodland and orchard walks).

Turn left to find the Tudor farmstead at Tregellast Barton, a working farm and now home to Roskilly's, a successful farm produce business, best known for its delicious icecream. Follow the lane past Roskilly's.

At the entrance to Trebarveth Farm 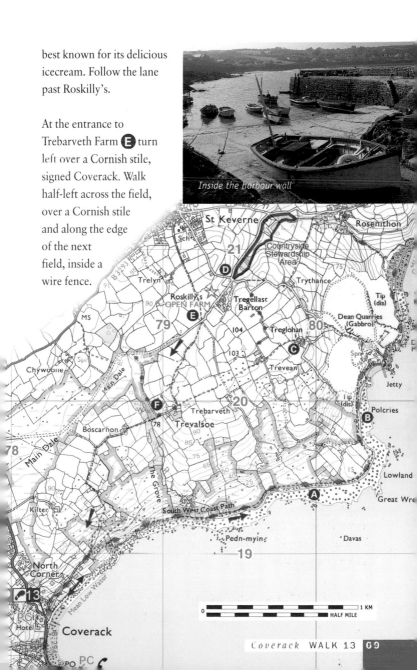 turn left over a Cornish stile, signed Coverack. Walk half-left across the field, over a Cornish stile and along the edge of the next field, inside a wire fence.

Inside the harbour wall

Boats in Coverack harbour

Go over another Cornish stile at the end and straight on, keeping the hedge on the left. Cross the next stile and keep straight on across the field, aiming for another hedgebank coming in from the left. Follow that hedgebank to leave the field over a Cornish stile; cross the next field diagonally, aiming for the top left corner. Leave over a Cornish stile; turn right down the lane at Trevalsoe.

Where the lane bends right **F**, turn left following a footpath post/arrow. Walk through a strip of woodland and over a stone stile to reach Boscarnon. Follow the track to the left of the house (note water trough for dogs) and walk down the drive, which becomes a concrete lane. Where the lane bends right, turn left over the stile in the hedgebank. Once in the field, walk left through a gap in the hedge and straight ahead over a stile. Walk ahead, aiming for a gate in the top right corner, to pass under big sycamore trees. Follow footpath signs through a kissing-gate into woodland, then through another into a scrubby area. The path becomes vague here but keep heading downhill, eventually bearing right over two stiles, with views of Coverack ahead. Rejoin the coast path and turn right; retrace the outward route to your car. ■

St Anthony-in-Meneage

- Riverside path
- sandy coves
- coastal headland
- beautiful church

Starting (or ending) at the characterful New Inn in peaceful Manaccan village, the route follows the edge of Helford River, with views across to the gardens at Trebah and Glendurgan, then runs around the end of Dennis Head to tucked-away St Anthony-in-Meneage, with its beautiful church. This walk can easily be done in either direction.

walk 14

Helford Passage

walk **14**

START Manaccan

DISTANCE 5 miles (8km)

TIME 2 hours

PARKING In the centre of Manaccan village, near the restored well

ROUTE FEATURES Relatively easy coast path; some paths muddy after rain; dogs to be kept on leads through Bosahan estate and farmland

GPS WAYPOINTS
🐾 SW 763 249
Ⓐ SW 763 260
Ⓑ SW 772 263
Ⓒ SW 786 256
Ⓓ SW 783 256
Ⓔ SW 771 251

PUBLIC TRANSPORT Bus service from Truro via Helston

REFRESHMENTS The New Inn and South Café, Manaccan; shop selling icecreams at St Anthony-in-Meneage (seasonal)

PUBLIC TOILETS None en route

PLAY AREA In Manaccan

ORDNANCE SURVEY MAPS Explorer 103 (The Lizard), Landranger 204 (Truro & Falmouth)

Walk up the lane towards Helford, passing the school and children's playground, to the crossroads. Walk straight over, and follow the quiet lane past Bosahan Barton and downhill towards Helford.

Where the lane bends sharp left Ⓐ, bear right down a narrow dead end lane signed Treath. Where that lane bends sharp left, turn right on the coast path (permissive path) through the Bosahan estate. Look across the Helford River towards the Ferry Boat Inn at Helford Passage. There has been a passenger ferry here since medieval times (when it belonged to the Bishops of Exeter). Until the

early years of the 20th century, horses and carts were also carried over, the horses having to swim beside the ferry. Helford village itself, a popular yet exclusive holiday venue, was for many years an important

The sheltered **Helford River** is blessed with three beautiful gardens, all of which are open to the public: Glendurgan, dating from the early 19th century and now in the hands of the National Trust; Trebah, which is privately owned; Carwinion, still a private home. These gardens contain many rare and exotic plants, and are known for their collections of camellias, rhododendrons and azaleas, all of which flourish in the mild climate. Glendurgan also has a spectacular laurel maze.

port, exporting tin and copper, as evidenced by the fact that the village had its own custom house.

The path – thick with snowdrops in February – leads behind Kennel Cottages (note the old kennels on the right). Look across the river to the pretty hamlet of Durgan, and the gardens at Trebah and Glendurgan.

Walk through woodland (bluebells in May) to reach the first of two private coves at Bosahan **B**, and then onto sandy Ponsence Cove (daffodils in early spring), popular with visitors who arrive by boat. Eventually the coast path passes through a kissing-gate into fields; look north east for views of

When was the well in the centre of Manaccan restored, and why?

St Mawes and St Anthony Lighthouse. Walk left along the field edge, cross a Cornish stile, and along the edge of the next field. Cross a narrow stile, and keep along the bottom of the next field, which is left via a wooden kissing-gate. Walk up the next field, keeping the hedge left, and pass through a kissing-gate. Keep up the left edge of the next field, with views over Gillan Creek to the right. Go through another kissing-gate and keep up the left edge of the field.

Turn left over a stile **C**. Take the first path left to wind around the end of Dennis Head. 'Dennis' derives from the Cornish 'dinas' (castle), and Iron Age earthworks here provide early evidence of the head's defensive position. The headland was fortified again during the Spanish Armada and Napoleonic wars, and was held by Royalists to protect the tin trade during the Civil War.

Continue around the head to reach the stile again. Turn right; pass through a stand of gorse, then bear half left diagonally down the field, which is left via a metal gate to reach a coast path sign.

Turn left to meet the lane **D**, then right to pass the church via the churchyard. Rejoin the lane and turn right, to walk inland up Gillan Creek, which can be crossed on foot at low tide. Eventually the lane descends gently and bears left, as the head of the creek at Carne comes into view.

Turn right as signed on a footpath and go through a gate **E**. Follow the often wet track uphill through woodland to pass through Roscaddon, then follow the drive all the way into Manaccan. On meeting a lane cross over and walk through the churchyard. Note the old fig tree that grows out of the church wall; it is said that anyone picking figs will experience bad luck and that the whole village will suffer should the tree be damaged. Leave the churchyard via a metal gate and turn left, then right by the post office and village shop and down a narrow path to your car. ∎

Mount Edgcumbe

■ Plymouth Sound   ■ Mount Edgcumbe gardens
■ wooded zigzag path   ■ Empacombe Harbour

*This is a walk of real contrasts: a fascinating
exploration of a peaceful and little-known corner of
Cornwall, far off the beaten track yet lying just across
the water from the bustling city of Plymouth, in Devon,
and easily accessible by ferry. The route goes through
the lovely Mount Edgcumbe Country Park and gardens,
with wonderful views across Plymouth Sound.*

walk 15

Picklecombe Fort, Mount Edgcumbe

walk **15**

START Maker church

DISTANCE 5½ miles (8.8km)

TIME 2½ hours

PARKING Country Park upper car park (closes 18.00), near Maker church

ROUTE FEATURES *Steep descent to Millbrook creek, sometimes slippery; part of coast path has steep ascent/descent (steps);* dogs on leads in Country Park, and to be kept under control at all times

GPS WAYPOINTS
  SX 447 520
Ⓐ SX 445 520
Ⓑ SX 442 524
Ⓒ SX 454 534
Ⓓ SX 458 524
Ⓔ SX 448 514
Ⓕ SX 440 517

PUBLIC TRANSPORT Bus service from Plymouth (to Cremyll only)

REFRESHMENTS Edgcumbe Inn at Cremyll, Orangery Restaurant in Mount Edgcumbe Gardens (daily in season 10.30–16.00), Friary Manor Hotel, Maker Heights (coffee, lunches, cream teas)

PUBLIC TOILETS At Cremyll, and near the Orangery Restaurant

PLAY AREA None

ORDNANCE SURVEY MAPS Explorer 108 (Lower Tamar Valley & Plymouth), Landranger 201 (Plymouth & Launceston)

Leave the car park out of the entrance, passing Maker church on the left, to reach a footpath post (signed Empacombe and Cremyll ferry) Ⓐ.

> **?** *What is the name of the Cremyll ferry?*

Turn right downhill to reach a wooden gate onto a lane; cross over and descend steps into woodland. Follow a yellow arrow right and turn immediately left downhill past a disused quarry (left), then follow footpath posts to the bottom of the woods. Turn left through a kissing-gate into a field. Walk straight on, with lovely views ahead to Torpoint, with Brunel's iron railway bridge over the Tamar at Saltash beyond. Join a track at the bottom of the field; go through a kissing-gate on to the lane Ⓑ.

Cross the lane and over the stile, with Millbrook Lake to the left. The level path runs along the field edge to pass through a kissing-gate. Walk along the bottom of the next field – note ruined windmill right – to enter woodland, and cross a stile to tranquil Empacombe Harbour, where the components for the second Eddystone lighthouse were put together in the early 17th century. Be sure to keep to the

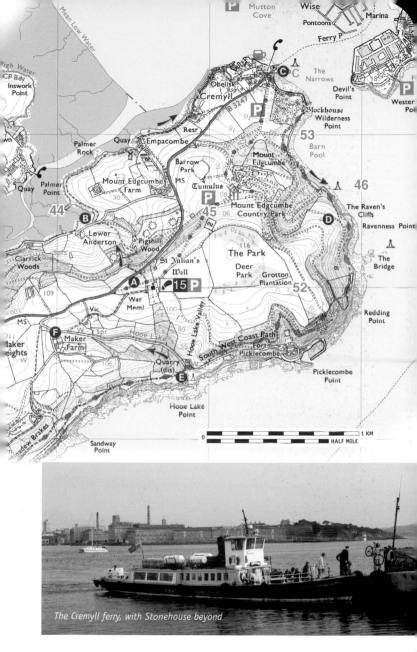

The Cremyll ferry, with Stonehouse beyond

waymarked route around the edge of the harbour, then to the left of Harbour Side House through a gateway. At the gate to Empacombe House (left) follow the wall ahead. Walk through an open gateway at the bottom of the next field; keep left through a kissing-gate to pass a derelict Admiralty pumping station. The path leads through another kissing-gate into an open field, and back into woodland. Cross a wide metal stile; look back right to see an 18th-century obelisk (navigation aid). The path runs into a track and meets the road at Cremyll (toilets right),

✳ The gardens and Country Park at **Mount Edgcumbe** are open all year round, and cover 860 acres. The formal gardens near Cremyll were laid out in the 18th century, as were the Earl's Garden near the house, and the Earl's Drive, which runs west from the house through the park to Penlee Point. The gardens are peppered with follies and grottos. The fallow deer that can sometimes be seen in the park are descendants of the herd originally established in the 16th century.

opposite the foot ferry **C**, with the monumental 19th-century Stonehouse Barracks over the water. The Edgcumbe Arms is to the left.

By the Orangery Restaurant

Turn right on the road (the coast path, though unsigned). Where the road bears right, walk straight ahead through the gates to Mount Edgcumbe Country Park (the small side gate is always open). Turn left; look right to see the house at the top end of a lovely horse-chestnut avenue. Pass through the gatehouse and the Orangery Restaurant; follow the path straight on to reach the seawall and a blockhouse (1540) near the battery at Wilderness Point. Walk on past the Great Hedge, an ilex hedge planted around 1700 to protect the gardens from salt spray. Pass through a gate to leave the formal gardens, and along the back of Barn Pool (used for tank embarkation during the Second World War invasion of France). Look across to Plymouth Hoe and Drake's Island (originally known as St Nicholas' Island, after its chapel), which once housed a prison, then re-enter woodland by Milton's Temple. Keep ahead to pass through a wooden gate into the Deer Park **D**.

Bear left on a small grassy path (coast path) and follow footpath posts along low cliffs and boardwalks to reach a steeply ascending zigzag path, with steps. Pass through a gate and by a folly. Soon after do not miss a small yellow sign left, the start of a zigzag route downhill to meet a woodland track. Follow this around the back of Picklecombe Point with its fort and quay. The track splits; keep left downhill to meet a lane through a kissing-gate **E**. The old smuggling villages of Kingsand and Cawsand can be seen ahead, lying either side of the pre-1844 Devon/Cornwall border; the place names on the Rame peninsula tend to be Old English rather than Cornish.

Turn right along the lane and climb steadily inland up the Hooe Lake Valley.

Just before Maker Farm, turn right through a gate, signed Maker church **F**. Cross the field and go through a kissing-gate; cross the next field, aiming for a gate/stile to the left of the house. Go straight on (garden right) through a wooden gate; cross a stile and turn immediately right along the hedgebank. Climb over a railed Cornish stile and turn right towards the church; rejoin the lane to the car park.

> **✻ Mount Edgcumbe House** was built from 1547–53 by Richard Edgcumbe of Cotehele, and was occupied by the Edgcumbe family until 1987. It was gutted by incendiary bombs on 22 April 1941, but the outer walls survived. The house was restored by Adrian Gilbert Scott between 1958–64, when the remaining red Tudor walls, granite window frames, 17th-century entrance door and 18th-century corner towers were incorporated into the fabric of the new building.

Morwenstow

- Hawker's Hut
- church and vicarage
- rolling farmalnd
- spectacular cliffs

The remote hamlet of Morwenstow, lying just 2 miles from the Devon border, is a gem, and well worth investigating. Do not be misled by the easy start to this walk, which runs across wooded combes and farmland to Stanbury Mouth: the return along the coast path is hard work, but the views and sense of space repay every ounce of effort.

Higher Sharpnose Point

walk **16**

START Church of St Morwenna & St John the Baptist, Morwenstow

DISTANCE 4½ miles (7.2km)

TIME 2½ hours

PARKING National Trust car park by the church (contributions cairn)

ROUTE FEATURES *Very steep ascents/descents on coast path and some exposed sections; dogs to be kept on lead through farmland, and under control at all times*

GPS WAYPOINTS

 SS 205 152
Ⓐ SS 208 151
Ⓑ SS 208 144
Ⓒ SS 211 136
Ⓓ SS 201 134
Ⓔ SS 196 147
Ⓕ SS 199 152

PUBLIC TRANSPORT Bus service from Bude and Holsworthy

REFRESHMENTS The Bush Inn at Crosstown; Rectory Farm Tearooms at Morwenstow

PUBLIC TOILETS Behind the church

PLAY AREA None

ORDNANCE SURVEY MAPS Explorer 126 (Clovelly & Hartland), Landranger 190 (Bude & Clovelly)

From the car park walk back up the lane to reach the green at Crosstown Ⓐ.

Turn right and walk through the gate to the right of The Bush Inn. Walk through the beer garden and go through a gap in the hedgebank in the bottom left corner. Pass through a kissing-gate to enter the Tidna Valley. Walk downhill to a kissing-gate leading into sycamore woodland, and down steps. Ignore the path straight ahead (to the coast path); turn left through a gate and cross the stream. Follow the path up the other side of the combe and through a gate; continue up a banked track and through a gate into a field. Keep ahead, with the hedgebank left, and go through the next gate. Cross the next field and enter a strip of woodland via a gate, then pass through another to hit the track to the right of ornamental gates leading to the medieval manor house at Tonacombe Ⓑ.

> ✱ Hawker's lovely church of **St Morwenna & St John the Baptist** (there are two holy wells dedicated to these saints nearby) is the most northerly parish church in Cornwall. It was enlarged in the 16th and 17th centuries, and its pinnacled tower provided a useful landmark from the sea in times past. There are three beautiful Norman arches in the nave, with typical zigzag moulding.

Cross the track and pass through a gate; walk up the middle of the field, through a gate/stile/gate into the next, and walk straight across the next, heading for a gate in the centre of a line of buildings at Stanbury Farm, with views of the incongruous Composite Signals Organisation Station at Cleave Camp ahead. Pass through the gate onto a lane. Turn left, and almost immediately right, down the drive to Stanbury; at the edge of the yard in front of the house turn left down a fenced track between ponds, to a field gate. Bear right to cross a Cornish stile and a wooden stile. Bear slightly left across the next field, and pass through a metal gate (do not go through the next metal gate **C** ahead, which leads onto the lane opposite the drive to Eastaway Manor).

Turn immediately sharp right, keeping the hedgebank on the right. Leave the field over a double stile, downhill across the next field, and over a stile into a wooded combe. Walk over the footbridge and through a gate; turn left down a rough path. Pass through a kissing-gate into the next field and straight on, then over a stile to meet a green lane on a bend. Keep ahead downhill; the lane (boggy in parts) ends at a gate; follow the narrow path downhill to meet the coast path **D**. (If you want to look at the beach, keep ahead on the coast path to cross a footbridge and scramble down to the rocky beach at Stanbury Mouth.) The coast from Bude to Hartland Point is a geologist's dream, a complex succession of vertical tiltings and contortions dating back some 300 million years. On reaching the coast path turn right steeply uphill, and then follow the path along the cliff edge. *Take care: for much of the way to Vicarage Cliff the cliffs are unstable.* Eventually cross two footbridges and a stile. The next stile leads onto Higher Sharpnose Point **E**; follow the path straight on to pass the old coastguard lookout, from where there are views to Hartland Quay to the north.

Follow the coast path steeply downhill to cross a stile and then a stream at Tidna Shute. The last sighting of the large blue butterfly, extinct since 1979, was in the Tidna Valley. Follow the coast path very steeply up onto

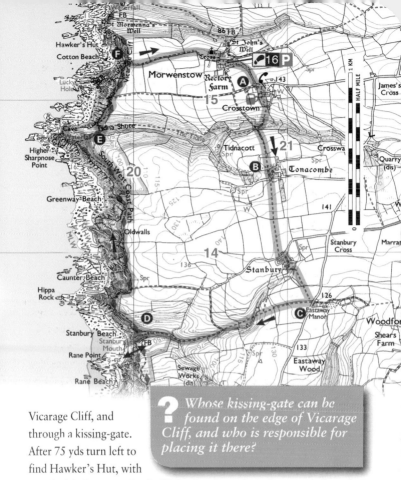

Vicarage Cliff, and
through a kissing-gate.
After 75 yds turn left to
find Hawker's Hut, with

? *Whose kissing-gate can be found on the edge of Vicarage Cliff, and who is responsible for placing it there?*

wonderful views over Lucky Hole. Continue along the coast path, and through a kissing-gate **F**.

Turn right inland. Go through two kissing-gates; where the hedgebank bears away right, cross the field towards the church, and over a Cornish stile into the churchyard. Take the path rising right from the south door, out through the lych gate, and back to the car. Look out for the ghostly white figurehead of the *Caledonia* to the right of the path, wrecked in 1842, which marks the graves of her captain and crew.

Lamorna and Mousehole

- ■ Wonderful cove
- ■ nature reserve
- ■ pretty fishing harbour
- ■ cliff terrace cultivation

A popular yet peaceful route along the undulating coast path from secluded Lamorna Cove to the quintessential Cornish fishing village of Mousehole, with its sheltered harbour and narrow, flower-filled alleyways and courts, perfect for a relaxing exploration on foot. This walk can easily be done in either direction; there is a clearly signed fee-paying car park in Mousehole.

Mousehole

walk **17**

START Lamorna Cove

DISTANCE 5 miles (8km)

TIME 3 hours

PARKING Car park (fee-paying) at the quay at Lamorna Cove

ROUTE FEATURES Scrambly coast path, with big rocks, steps and wet patches; *steep descent to/ascent from Mousehole on lane;* inland fields boggy in wet weather, especially round farms; dogs to be kept under control at all times and on leads through farmland

GPS WAYPOINTS

    SW 450 241
Ⓐ SW 457 239
Ⓑ SW 466 256
Ⓒ SW 469 262
Ⓓ SW 466 255
Ⓔ SW 464 254
Ⓕ SW 458 249

PUBLIC TRANSPORT None available

REFRESHMENTS Lamorna Wink pub and café at Lamorna Cove; pubs and seasonal cafés in Mousehole

PUBLIC TOILETS At Lamorna Cove; by the harbour in Mousehole

PLAY AREA None

ORDNANCE SURVEY MAPS Explorer 102 (Land's End), Landranger 203 (Land's End & Isles of Scilly)

* Tragically, the village of **Mousehole** hit the headlines just before Christmas in 1981 when the entire crew of the Penlee lifeboat – *Solomon Browne* – was lost while attempting to save the crew of the cargo vessel the *Union Star*, which was wrecked below Boscawen Point to the west of Lamorna Cove. This sad event is commemorated by a garden at the lifeboat house, and by a memorial at the church of St Paul de Leon at Paul, on the way to Newlyn.*

From the quay, walk a few steps inland, then turn right to walk in front of the row of cottages, with their gardens between the path and the sea. Cross the stream (public toilets to the left) and follow the rocky coast path past the granite quarry on the left, and walk on to the craggy headland at Carn-du **Ⓐ**, pink with sea thrift in May, from where there are superb views back to the cove.

The path continues down rough granite steps to run along the level low-lying Kemyel Cliff, then passes into Kemyel Crease Nature Reserve, owned by the Cornwall Wildlife Trust since 1974, and a haven for insects, butterflies and birds. This sheltered, frost-free part of the Cornish coast, between here and Mousehole, has long been terraced for the cultivation of bulbs. Daffodils were grown for the

Lamorna Cove

London markets, and potatoes were cultivated here during the Second World War. As a result, much of the existing vegetation has a 'civilised' feel, with Monterey pines (unique to this part of the coast, and so a familiar landmark for passing vessels), fuchsias, hydrangeas, violets and daffodils in season. The next part of the coast path, as far as the disused coastguard lookout on Penzer Point, is extremely undulating, with many stepped ascents and descents before ascending over Penzer Point. Eventually the path levels and runs inland a little to meet a gritty track. Porth Enys House, on the right, overlooks Point Spaniard, where the Spaniards landed in 1595 before destroying Mousehole, Paul, Newlyn and Penzance. It is said that only one building in Mousehole survived: the Keigwin Arms, now a private house, but restored in Elizabethan manor house style.

B Turn right; follow the lane steeply down into Mousehole. Just past the huge Weslyan church on the left, turn right to have a look at the harbour (public toilets right) **C**. It's not hard to understand why

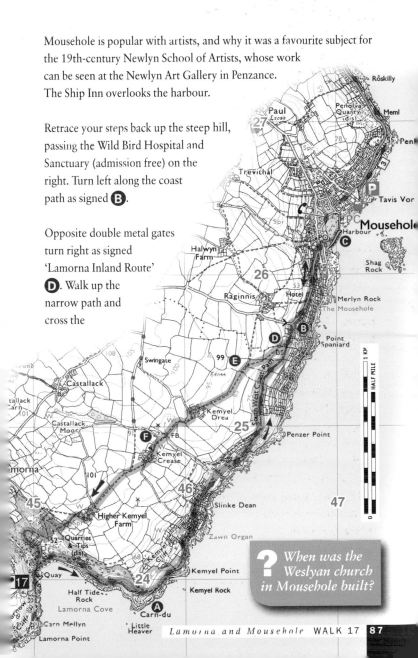

Mousehole is popular with artists, and why it was a favourite subject for the 19th-century Newlyn School of Artists, whose work can be seen at the Newlyn Art Gallery in Penzance. The Ship Inn overlooks the harbour.

Retrace your steps back up the steep hill, passing the Wild Bird Hospital and Sanctuary (admission free) on the right. Turn left along the coast path as signed **B**.

Opposite double metal gates turn right as signed 'Lamorna Inland Route' **D**. Walk up the narrow path and cross the

? *When was the Weslyan church in Mousehole built?*

Lamorna and Mousehole WALK 17 **87**

hedgebank. Cross the next field diagonally, aiming for the top corner, and cross the next hedgebank. Walk diagonally up the next field and over a Cornish stile at the top **E**.

Keep along the top right edge of three fields and then cross a stone stile to reach the farm at Kemyel Drea (very muddy in winter). Keep ahead as signed, passing between farm buildings via four gates and a Cornish stile. Follow the footpath sign left, then bear right as signed to cross a grassy corner. Join a signed path, which bears right between high hedgebanks. The path continues across boggy ground, eventually on stone slabs, crosses a stile, then another into a field. Keeping the hedge on the right, leave at the top of the field via a stone stile **F**.

Mousehole harbour in the summer

Turn left on the lane by Kemyel House. Follow the lane through Kemyel Crease Farm, where it degrades to a track. Follow the footpath sign right up and over the hedgebank, and make for a footpath post on the hedgebank corner ahead. From there head for a Cornish stile across the next bank, keep ahead to cross another, then head towards Kemyel Wartha, keeping the hedgebank right. Cross a stile to reach the track by the buildings, then follow footpath signs left. The track passes to the left of some converted farm buildings; where the track bends right keep straight ahead on a grassy track. Where the path is signed both ahead and left, turn left between high hedges. As the top of Lamorna Cove is reached, follow the path down past the quarry, then zigzag downhill to rejoin the coast path. Turn right to cross the stream, then left for your car. ∎

St Anthony Head

■ Tidal creek ■ wildflowers and seabirds
■ sailing boats ■ lighthouse and toposcope

A long yet not strenuous walk which takes in some of the best features of the south Cornwall coast: great views across the River Fal to St Mawes with its 16th-century castle, and Falmouth beyond; stunning Place House and church of St Anthony-in-Roseland; the beautiful coast path to St Anthony Head, with its lighthouse and battery; and golden sandy beaches at Porthbeor and Porth.

walk 18

Place House

walk 18

START Porth Farm top car park

DISTANCE 6½ miles (10.5km)

TIME 3 hours

PARKING Two National Trust car parks at Porth Farm (£2 honesty box)

ROUTE FEATURES Some paths muddy after wet weather; some dog-friendly stiles on coast path, some not; dogs on leads through Place conservation area; *very steep climb from St Anthony lighthouse to* **E**

GPS WAYPOINTS
- 🥾 SW 867 329
- **Ⓐ** SW 867 330
- **Ⓑ** SW 855 322
- **Ⓒ** SW 856 320
- **Ⓓ** SW 851 322
- **Ⓔ** SW 847 313
- **Ⓕ** SW 861 320
- **Ⓖ** SW 869 329

PUBLIC TRANSPORT None available)

REFRESHMENTS Royal Standard pub at Gerrans, Plume of Feathers pub and The Boathouse Restaurant in Portscatho, both north of Porth

PUBLIC TOILETS At St Anthony Head, and opposite Porth Farm

PLAY AREA None

ORDNANCE SURVEY MAPS Explorer 105 (Falmouth & Mevagissey), Landranger 204 (Truro & Falmouth)

👣 From the upper car park entrance turn left on the lane and left again at Porth Farm. At the lower car park entrance follow the footpath sign right, signed Percuil (Porthcuel) River and Place, through woodland.

The path turns left over a railed footbridge **Ⓐ**, passes through a gate and then runs right along the bottom edge of a field, with Porth Creek to the right. Go through a gate and follow the narrow, rooty path through deciduous woodland. Ignore a sign left to Bohortha and follow the path as it bears left along the Percuil

✳ The tip of the **Roseland Peninsula** ('ros' is Cornish for promontory), bounded by the Carrick Roads and River Fal on the west, and by Veryan Bay and Gerrans Bay on the east, has been a site of great strategic importance for hundreds of years, guarding the entrance to the great natural harbour of the Carrick Roads. Most of what can be seen at St Anthony Battery dates from the end of the 19th century, much now tastefully converted into holiday accommodation by the National Trust, which took over the site in 1959.

River, with views across to St Mawes, a popular sailing centre, and headquarters of the Roseland Gig Club (the club's

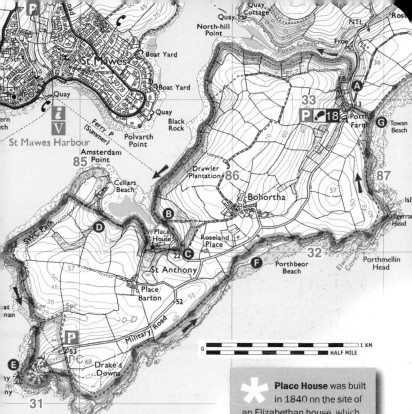

oldest gig, the *Newquay*, was built in 1812) opposite. After a long wooded stretch, the path crosses a stile to enter a field, then crosses another stile back into woodland again. Ignore another path to Bohortha (left). Views of Henry VIII's impressive 16th-century St Mawes Castle, with Falmouth beyond, open up to the right. Walk past St Mawes ferry point at Totty's

Place House was built in 1840 on the site of an Elizabethan house, which itself replaced an earlier priory. The lovely little church of St Anthony-in-Roseland is joined to the house by the north transcept, and has a superb Norman south door. The church is a rare survival in that it avoided the widespread restoration and rebuilding of many Cornish churches in the 15th century. There was probably a small church here in the mid-10th century, and the place does have a wonderfully ancient feel.

looking towards St Anthony Head Lighthouse

Steps (at high water the ferry lands at Place Quay), through a kissing-gate, along a field edge and through another kissing-gate to gain the lane at Place Quay **B**, with splendid Place House opposite.

Turn up the lane, with great views of the sweeping lawns in front of Place House on the right, formerly the site of a mill pond. Walk up the lane, passing The Lodge (left) and Lavender Cottage (right).

Turn right over a stone stile **C**, following coast path signs to St Anthony Head. The path leads through the atmospheric graveyard of the beautiful 12th/13th-century church of St Anthony-in-Roseland. Follow the path up stone steps from the south door of the church to pass an old orchard on the left, then right to join a broad track. Keep right and follow the track along the back of Place House, then along Cellars Beach. The cottages ahead (now holiday accommodation) were formerly pilchard cellars, where the catch was processed for export to the Catholic countries of Europe.

Turn left through a gate **D** to leave the track, signed St Anthony Head, and walk up the right edge of the field. Pass through a kissing-gate at the top with fantastic views of St Mawes and Pendennis castles ahead. Walk straight on very steeply downhill, then turn left to walk along low cliffs. Leave the field via a kissing-gate, and follow the path round Carricknath Point, then through a kissing-gate, before dropping steeply down through a gate and over a wooden walkway at the back of Great Molunan beach, a great spot for picnics and rock-pooling. Follow the coast path right to pass through a white gate onto St Anthony Head

(National Trust). Where the coast path bends sharp left and uphill, walk straight on to have a look at the lighthouse (now holiday accommodation), built in 1834 (though a beacon had been burnt here for many years before then) to warn mariners of the dangers of The Manacles reef and to watch over the entrance to the Carrick Roads. From 1882 a large bell (the largest in Cornwall) was rung in foggy conditions, replaced by a fog-horn in 1954. Retrace your steps and follow the coast path very steeply uphill, eventually ascending steps, to reach the car park at St Anthony Battery **E**.

Turn right to walk past the converted officers' quarters; opposite Tiffy's take the tarmac path around the end of the point past the gun emplacements and toposcope, and above the Second World War observation post. The path passes through some defensive earthworks, and leads on round Zone Point, with views to Porthbeor beach ahead. This stretch of the coast is good for spotting fulmar and gannets. Pass through a gate, and later over a Cornish stile (particularly non-dog-friendly!) before crossing another onto National Trust land at Porthbeor **F**.

Walk above Porthbeor beach. Pass through a gate and continue past Elwinick Cove; cross a stile onto Porthmellin and then Killigerran Heads – the coastal grassland is particularly lovely here, ecologically managed and supporting a wide range of wildflowers – before descending to long, low-lying Towan beach ('towan' is Cornish for sand dune). Pass through a gate; note the wreck post on the right, erected by the coastguard service and used to simulate a ship's mast in training exercises. Turn left at the back of the beach **G** and walk inland on an old sanding road, used in the past to transport seaweed from the beach by donkey and packhorse, for use as fertiliser. Bear left to pass through through a National Trust building housing toilets, to reach the road opposite Porth Farm. ▪

> **?** *What was stored in the small white building to the right of the coast path after Great Molunan beach?*

Trevone and Stepper Point

■ Tortured coastline   ■ sweeping estuary views
■ daymark   ■ fascinating geology

walk 19

The section of coast between Trevone and Stepper Point is characterised by dramatic, tortured slate cliffs and wide-ranging views towards Pentire Point. But this is a walk of contrasts: the second part, turning inland along the edge of the broad sweep of the Camel Estuary, feels calm and safe by comparison, as does the return to Trevone across rolling arable farmland via the hamlet of Crugmeer.

Sandy Harbour Cove, with Hawker's Cove beyond

walk 19

START Trevone Bay

DISTANCE 6½ miles (10.5km)

TIME 3 hours

PARKING Beach Complex car park (fee-paying in season) to left of Trevone beach

ROUTE FEATURES *Take care on coast path Trevone to Stepper Point (unfenced and high cliffs); beware Round Hole at Trevone, dogs on leads; non-dog-friendly high Cornish stiles*

GPS WAYPOINTS

📷 SW 891 759
🅐 SW 892 760
🅑 SW 895 770
🅒 SW 907 778
🅓 SW 910 784
🅔 SW 911 768
🅕 SW 912 760
🅖 SW 902 765

PUBLIC TRANSPORT Bus service from Newquay, Padstow, St Columb Major (to Windmill on B3276 1 mile from start)

REFRESHMENTS Madrips beach café at Trevone beach; Well Parc pub in Trevone; tearoom at Prideaux Place (March – October; small charge to enter grounds)

PUBLIC TOILETS At Trevone beach

PLAY AREA None

ORDNANCE SURVEY MAPS Explorer 106 (Newquay & Padstow), Landranger 200 (Newquay & Bodmin)

📷 Pick up coast path signs at the left end of the car park and cross the top of the beach.

> **?** *How large an area does the Stepper Point access area cover?*

Follow coast path signs up concrete steps 🅐 onto the open cliff, and walk around the end of Round Hole Point. The Round Hole itself, a collapsed sea cave, lies a little inland up the cliff. There is a huge contrast here between the view over the sandy beach at Trevone, to the south-west, and the magnificent, unforgiving, indented coastline ahead. The path runs along a broad, level, grassy section of cliff to pass an unusual area of limestone cliff at Marble Cliff, Porthmissen: most of the north Cornwall coast is composed of slate, with headlands formed of resistant igneous rock. The path runs along the back of Longcarrow Cove, then over a Cornish stile, before dropping steeply down to cross a small combe on a wooden footbridge. Cross a railed Cornish stile and walk up the other side of the combe. It then drops steeply downhill again to cross another small combe. Follow coast path posts straight up the cliff (*this is very steep*) to meet the next footpath post at the top overlooking the detached sections of cliff that have formed the extraordinarily contorted Lower, Middle and Higher Merope islands **B**. *Note: extreme care should be taken here.*

✱ **Prideaux Place** was built by the Prideaux family in the 16th century and is now occupied by their descendants. Surrounded by beautiful gardens, mainly laid out in Georgian and Victorian times, the estate also boasts a deer park dating from 1750; legend has it that if the deer were ever to die out that would herald the end of the Prideaux family. A tunnel leads from the grounds to the 13th/14th-century St Petroc's Church, giving the family private access to Padstow's main place of worship.

Follow the coast path as it levels out and runs along the cliffs towards Butter Hole, crossing a Cornish stile en route. Look out for fulmar, razorbill and guillemot offshore. The path drops down to pass through a kissing-gate to enter the Stepper Point access area **C**.

Stepper Point is composed of greenstone, and, in the past, has been heavily quarried for roadstone. Cross the next stile, then reach a kissing-gate at the back of Butter Hole: look out for the fantastic green and purple bands of slate in the cliff-face here. Follow the path around the back of the cove, and footpath posts onto Stepper Point to reach the Pepperpot **D**, a daymark constructed in 1832 by the Association for the Preservation of Life and Property. There are wonderful views from here up the expansive Camel Estuary, and across Padstow Bay to Polzeath and beyond.

From the daymark, follow the coast path ahead. The next coast path sign directs you right through the broken-down hedgebank near St John's Well.

Leave Stepper Point over a stile and follow the Camel Estuary inland, with superb views over Daymer Bay and Brae Hill, where on summer evenings you can listen to readings of Sir John's Betjeman's poetry. He is buried at St Enodoc Church, which can be spotted peeping out from the sand dunes just to the left of Brae Hill. Walk through the next kissing-gate; the path becomes narrow and gritty (wonderful blackberries in September), to reach Hawker's Cove via another kissing-gate. The older property here was built in 1847 to house the pilots who helped vessels negotiate the notorious and potentially lethal Doom Bar, a shifting sandbank across the estuary responsible for more than 300 shipwrecks from 1760 to

The daymark on Stepper Point

1920; the other cottages were built for coastguards.

Follow coast path signs around the back of the cove past the slipway, to rejoin the lane and turn left, and over a wooden stile to continue on a gritty path past the old lifeboat station, built in 1827. Shifting sands rendered it unusable, and in 1967 the Padstow lifeboat moved west to Mother Ivey's Bay. Continue over a Cornish stile to reach the back of Sandy Harbour Cove, where boats were moored until the 1920s when the main navigation channel down the estuary moved out of reach. The path runs inland to cross a track and then a boardwalk. Cross the next stile and keep left along the field edge; pass the next stile and boardwalk onto a track; turn right.

Where the coast path is signed left **E**, go straight ahead uphill on a track (yellow arrow); at the top of the field turn right over a stile to Tregirls Farm. Turn left up the drive, which soon becomes tarmac; follow the lane over the brow of the hill.

Turn right over a stile **F** (for Prideaux Place keep straight on) and walk diagonally right across the field. Cross the farm track and go over the stile, and diagonally left across the next field. Over the next two stiles, and diagonally left across the next field, and over four more stiles to reach a track on the edge of Crugmeer **G**.

Turn left; at the T-junction turn right then left down a gritty lane which eventually runs downhill past Porthmissen to reach the car park at Trevone. ∎

Port Quin to Port Isaac

- ■ Rocky coves
- ■ rolling farmland
- ■ historic fishing village
- ■ coast path

Port Quin and Port Isaac are two of Cornwall's gems: the walk starts from the old pilchard-fishing hamlet of Port Quin, now in the hands of the National Trust, and leads to peaceful Port Isaac, one of the north coast's few reasonable natural harbours, before returning along a particularly beautiful yet tough stretch of the coastal footpath. Not a walk for the faint-hearted.

walk 20

Peaceful Port Quin

walk **20**

START Port Quin

DISTANCE 6½ miles (10.5km)

TIME 3 hours

PARKING National Trust car park at Port Quin (contributions cairn)

ROUTE FEATURES Dogs to be kept on leads through farmland; *strenuous coast path, with steep ascents/descents and long flights of high steps; parts slippery after rain*

GPS WAYPOINTS

🥾 SW 971 805
Ⓐ SW 973 805
Ⓑ SW 987 805
Ⓒ SW 995 808
Ⓓ SW 996 807
Ⓔ SW 989 808
Ⓕ SW 970 811

PUBLIC TRANSPORT None available)

REFRESHMENTS The Golden Lion pub and plentiful cafés and restaurants in Port Isaac; picnic tables at Port Quin

PUBLIC TOILETS In Port Isaac

PLAY AREA None

ORDNANCE SURVEY MAPS Explorer 106 (Newquay & Padstow), Landranger 200 (Newquay & Bodmin)

🥾 Walk out of the car park and turn right uphill away from the sea.

About 100 yds up the lane bear left, following footpath signs for Port Isaac Ⓐ, to pass in front of Howard's Cottage. Go over a Cornish stile by a white gate and into the field. Walk up the valley (boggy in winter); eventually the path bears uphill slightly left. At the top of the field pass over a Cornish stile between two five-bar gates. Walk along the track through large, sweeping arable fields: any sense of being anywhere near the sea is soon left far behind. Pass over the next two stiles, keeping on the track; look left for views of Tintagel along the coast. Cross over another stile just level with Roscarrock Farm Ⓑ.

Turn left along the left edge of the field to the bottom; follow the hedgebank right, and turn left over a wooden stile; look left for views of Pine Haven. The narrow path winds steeply downhill to reach the bottom of the combe. Turn left over a wooden railed footbridge, then over a big Cornish stile (ignoring the path to the coast path on the left) and keep ahead steeply uphill through brambles and gorse and out of the combe. The path leads into a field; keep straight ahead, passing to the left of an old wreck post on the hill ahead. Walk straight ahead and over a Cornish stile, with

The hamlet of **Port Quin** lies on a small natural harbour. There are disused antimony mines to the west, above Gibson's Cove. Mining supplemented the income gained from pilchard pressing and salting which took place in the old buildings behind the rocky cove, many of which have now been converted into holiday accommodation by the National Trust. Some know Port Quin as 'the village that died': legend has it that every local man perished in one shipwreck in the 19th century.

views of Port Isaac directly ahead. Pick your way down the edge of the next field, keeping the hedge on the left. The path leads over a slate slab

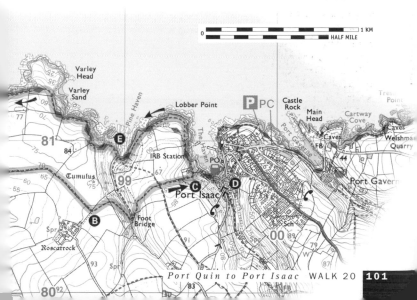

and downhill to emerge on to a tarmac track (the coast path) at the top of Roscarrock Hill **C**.

Turn right and walk steeply downhill into the centre of Port Isaac **D**, passing the toilets on the left at the bottom of the hill, and the pottery in the old chapel on the right. One of Port Isaac's major advantages is that the narrow, twisty streets make parking almost impossible, and visitors tend to use the car park at the top of the hill and walk in. Those who do park on the beach below the Platt at low tide always run the risk of getting the time wrong and returning to their car just that little bit too late.

Port Isaac's Cornish name – 'porth izic' – corn port – gives one clue as to what once went on in this unspoilt fishing village, which has been a working fishing harbour since the Middle Ages, and which still sends out working crabbers. There is still a sense of antiquity here, and the village has been used as a location for the film *Saving Grace* and more recently the TV series *Doc Marten*. It's an extremely picturesque place, with old pilchard cellars and slate-hung cottages crowded around narrow passageways, or 'drangs': don't miss the appropriately named Squeezee Belly alley.

Having explored the village and prepared yourself for the return route, retrace your steps to the top of Roscarrock Hill **C**, with perfect views over the harbour. Keep on the coast path as it runs in front of the last houses on the left, and up steps onto the open cliff. The path levels as it passes through a gap in a hedgebank, then runs round the edge of Lobber Point. Views of Port Isaac are quickly lost, on account of its incredibly sheltered location. The path descends to pretty Pine Haven and passes through a kissing-gate, signed Port Quin **E**.

Cross the stream via a wooden bridge, then climb two long flights of steps up the other side of the combe. Follow the path to reach Varley Head, and through a kissing-gate to cross the neck of the head; pass through another kissing-gate behind Greengarden Cove. *Note: much of*

Cornish stile above Port Isaac

this stretch of the coast path is unfenced, and caution should be exercised at all times. From here, the switchback coast path can be seen running all the way along to

> **?** How many steps are there in the two flights ascending after leaving Pine Cove on the coast path?

Kellan Head, and this is where the hard work really begins, with many steep ascents and descents, and a horrible number of steps – but it is worth it. Once Kellan Head is reached, there are lovely views of Doyden Castle on Doyden Point ahead: this folly, now in the care of the National Trust and available as holiday accommodation, was built soon after Samuel Symmons bought the headland in 1827, so that he could provide a suitable venue for a bit of out-of-the-way drinking and gambling with his colleagues.

From Kellan Head **F** follow the coast path as it runs inland (with several more flights of steps) to reach the top of the slipway at Port Quin; note the drinking-water tap on the wall opposite, which you may well be in need of at this point. Turn left to regain the car park. ∎

Further Information

Walking Safety

The walks in this book cover a varied range of landscapes. Whereas
most are set in reasonably gentle countryside that offers no real
dangers to walkers at any time of year, extra care should always be
exercised on any route that follows sections of the South West Coast
Path. Wherever you walk, it is still advisable to take sensible walking
precautions and follow certain well-tried guidelines.

Always take with you both warm and waterproof clothing and
sufficient food and drink. Wear suitable footwear, such as strong
walking boots or shoes that give a good grip over stony ground, on
slippery slopes and in muddy conditions. Try to obtain a local weather
forecast and bear it in mind before you start. Do not be afraid to
abandon your proposed route and return to your starting point in
the event of a sudden and unexpected deterioration in the weather.

All the walks described in this book will be safe to do, given due care
and respect, even during the winter. Indeed, a crisp, fine winter day
often provides perfect walking conditions, with firm ground
underfoot and a clarity unique to this time of the year.

The most difficult hazard likely to be encountered is mud, especially
when walking along woodland and field paths, farm tracks and
bridleways – the latter in particular can often get churned up by
cyclists and horses. In summer, an additional difficulty may be
narrow and overgrown paths, particularly along the edges of
cultivated fields. Neither should constitute a major problem
provided that the appropriate footwear is worn.

Port Isaac from the coast path

Global Positioning System (GPS)

What is GPS?

Global Positioning System, or GPS for short, is a fully-functional navigation system that uses a network of satellites to calculate positions, which are then transmitted to hand-held receivers. By measuring the time it takes a signal to reach the receiver, the distance from the satellite can be estimated. Repeat this with several satellites and the receiver can then triangulate its position, in effect telling the receiver exactly where you are, in any weather, day or night, anywhere on Earth.

GPS information, in the form of grid reference data, is increasingly being used in Pathfinder® guidebooks, and many readers find the positional accuracy GPS affords a reassurance, although its greatest benefit comes when you are walking in remote, open countryside or through forests.

GPS has become a vital global utility, indispensable for modern navigation on land, sea and air around the world, as well as an important tool for map-making and land surveying.

Follow the Country Code

- Be safe – plan ahead and follow any signs
- Leave gates and property as you find them
- Protect plants and animals, and take your litter home
- Keep dogs under close control
- Consider other people

(Natural England)

Hawker's Cove

Useful Organisations

Campaign to Protect Rural England
CPRE National Office,
128 Southwark Street,
London SE1 0SW
Tel. 020 7981 2800
www.cpre.org.uk

Cornwall Tourist Board
Visit Cornwall
Cornwall Enterprise
Pydar House, Pydar Street,
Truro TR1 1EA
Tel. 01872 322 800
www.visitcornwall.com

English Heritage
Customer Services Department,
PO Box 569, Swindon SN2 2YP
Tel. 0870 333 1181
www.english-heritage.org.uk

English Nature
Northminster House,
Peterborough,
Cambridgeshire PE1 1UA
Tel. 01733 455000
www.english-nature.org.uk

National Trust
Cornwall Regional Office
Lanydrock, Bodmin PL30 4DE

Tel. 01208 74281
www.nationaltrust.org.uk

Natural England
Block 3, Government Buildings,
Burghill Road,
Westbury on Trym,
Bristol BS10 6NJ
Tel. 0117 959 1000
www.naturalengland.org.uk

Ordnance Survey
Romsey Road, Maybush,
Southampton SO16 4GU
Tel. 08456 05 05 05 (Lo-call)
www.ordnancesurvey.co.uk

Public Transport
For all public transport enquiries
in Southwest England
Tel. 0871 200 2233
www.traveline.org.uk

National Rail Enquiries
Tel. 08457 484950
www.nationalrail.co.uk

Ramblers' Association
2nd Floor, Camelford House,
87-90 Albert Embankment,
London SE1 7TW
Tel. 020 7339 8500
www.ramblers.org.uk

Royal Society for the Protection of Birds (RSPB)
The Lodge, Sandy, Bedfordshire SG19 2DL
Tel. 01767 680551
www.rspb.org.uk

South West Coast Path Association
Bowker House, Lee Mill Bridge, Ivybridge, Devon PL21 9EF
Tel. 01752 896 237
www.swcp.org.uk

Youth Hostel Association
Trevelyan House, Dimple Road, Matlock, Derbyshire DE4 3YH
Tel. 01629 592700
www.yha.org.uk

Gorse and heather at Wheal Coates

Ordnance Survey maps of Cornwall

Explorer maps:	102 (Land's End)
	103 (The Lizard)
	104 (Redruth & St Agnes)
	105 (Falmouth & Mevagissey)
	106 (Newquay & Padstow)
	107 (St Austell & Liskeard)
	108 (Lower Tamar Valley & Plymouth)
	111 (Bude, Boscastle & Tintagel)
	112 (Launceston & Holsworthy)
	126 (Clovelly & Hartland)
Landranger maps:	190 (Bude & Clovelly)
	200 (Newquay & Bodmin)
	201 (Plymouth & Launceston)
	203 (Land's End & Isles of Scilly)
	204 (Truro & Falmouth)

Answers to Questions

Walk 1: He drowned while bathing near Land's End on Saturday 19 May, 1894.

Walk 2: It is the holy well of St Ia and, until 1843, formed the main water supply for Downalong (this part of St Ives).

Walk 3: The company helped in the restoration of the estate's woodlands after the great storm of 25 January 1990 (the seat is passed on the way to Garden Cottage).

Walk 4: By G. James Allday in 1951 (information available on a plaque just before the gate leading into Covington Wood).

Walk 5: It was manufactured by Sara & Sons of Redruth (wording on the side of lamppost).

Walk 6: Every 20 minutes.

Walk 7: In 1896, 'by public subscription for the use and enjoyment of the nation' (information available on an engraved stone to the right of the coast path on the way to Barras Nose).

Walk 8: 620ft (189m) (information available at the trig point on top of the beacon).

Walk 9: The *Ardgarry* and her crew of 12 (engraved on a granite memorial at Kilcobben Cove).

Walk 10: Rev Samuel J.P. Trist; it was restored in 1912 to commemorate the coronation of King George V and Queen Mary.

Walk 11: In 1870 (details on a plaque on the white pyramid seen during point ❸ of the walk).

Walk 12: The Mexico shaft is dedicated to Cornish miners and engineers who worked in Mexico 1824 – 1917 (found on a plaque at the end of the tarmac way below the café at Geevor).

Walk 13: Between 10.00 and 18.30; the warning is given by the flying of red flags, and a continuous blast on the hooter (information available on a notice at the edge of the quarry).

Walk 14: In 1977, for Queen Elizabeth II's Silver Jubilee.

Walk 15: *The Northern Belle.*

Walk 16: Edna's; placed there by Ronald, Gillian and Richard (inscription on the kissing-gate just before the path leading to Hawker's Hut).

Walk 17: 1905.

Walk 18: Paraffin; this is where paraffin for the lighthouse at St Anthony Head used to be kept.

Walk 19: A total of 138 acres – information available on a noticeboard at the entrance to the access area.

Walk 20: 148 + 29 = 177.

Crimson Walking Guides

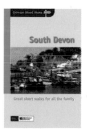

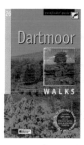

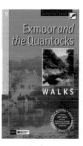
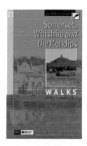
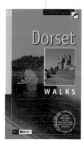
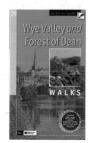
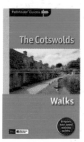
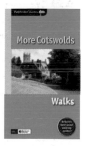

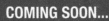